W9-CJI-231

DISCARDED

BLACKS IN CENTRAL AMERICA
BY SANTIAGO VALENCIA CHALÁ

BLACKS IN CENTRAL AMERICA
BY SANTIAGO VALENCIA CHALÁ

Translated from Spanish by
Niza Fabre

The Edwin Mellen Press
Lewiston•Queenston•Lampeter

Library of Congress Cataloging-in-Publication Data

Chalá, Santiago Valencia.
　Blacks in Central America by Santiago Valencia Chalá / translated from Spanish into English by Niza Fabre.
　　p. cm.
　Includes bibliographical references and index.
　ISBN-13: 978-0-7734-5762-1
　ISBN-10: 0-7734-5762-3
　I. Title.

hors série.

A CIP catalog record for this book is available from the British Library.

Copyright　©　2006　Niza Fabre

All rights reserved. For information contact

The Edwin Mellen Press Box 450 Lewiston, New York USA 14092-0450	The Edwin Mellen Press Box 67 Queenston, Ontario CANADA L0S 1L0

The Edwin Mellen Press, Ltd.
Lampeter, Ceredigion, Wales
UNITED KINGDOM SA48 8LT

Printed in the United States of America

**To the memory of Angelo Tarallo
(1940-2003)**

TABLE OF CONTENTS

PREFACE

This valuable work *Blacks in Central America* by Santiago Valencia Chalá and translated by Dr. Niza Fabre further validates and authenticates the history of African presence and the creolization of these mammoth cultural and linguistic forces on indigenous peoples of the Diaspora with particular foci here on the Caribbean and Central America. This eight chapter book is not only readable and accessible, but as a scholarly text paints an introductory sketch of the history of Blacks in Belize, Guatemala, Honduras, Nicaragua, Costa Rica and Panama. Indeed, this represents an ambitious undertaking and a panoramic overview of the acculturative processes that have shaped these countries and their national identities and is referred to as Garifuna culture.

The centrality of a spiritual life in the cosmology of the Garifuna is well documented in the second chapter. Bypassing the traditional belief system of a monotheistic God as defined by the Roman Catholic religion, the Garifunas embraced the dualistic concepts of African and Indian rites of ascension into the state of deification. The division of the human soul into three parts, that of Anigi (animal spirit), Iuani (soul), and Afurugu (supernatural) allow the individual's final journey to its resting place. Surviving relatives are an integral part of this voyage as they are kept abreast through visions and premonitions. This forged connection between the living and dead ties the two worlds together and validates the African worldview and ethos in Garifuna culture and traditions. The Garifunas of Belize date back to 1802 and their relationship described by Valencia Chalá with the English colonial administrators was tense. Despite threats of expulsion, they initially settled in Stan Creek and Dangrida. A number of the traditions are being maintained, and the need of Afro-Belizeans to forge connections with other communities across the Central American region is a growing phenomenon.

The foregoing discussion represents some of the cerebrally good discussions in this book. The other chapters provide a thumbnail historical and contemporary portrayal of Blacks in other Central American countries.

This work adds to the voluminous interdisciplinary work of the centrality of Africa within Latin America. This legacy is permanently etched and imprinted and is so visibly manifested in routine cultural traditions. It is certainly a welcomed and enjoyable read!

Dr. Virginia Gonsalves-Domond
Convener (chair) Africana-American Studies &
Associate Professor of Psychology
School of Social Sciences and Human Services
Ramapo College of New Jersey

ACKNOWLEDGMENTS

I would like to acknowledge with thanks and deep appreciation the assistance of Angelo Tarallo in reviewing and editing my English translation.

I would also like to thank Father Martín José Balda director of the Centro Cultural Afro-Ecuatoriano for granting permission for this translation.

My special thanks to my Africana Studies Colleagues from Ramapo College, School of Social Sciences and Human Services, Virginia Gonsalves Domond, Karl Johnson, and Sam Pinn for their support, for reading the manuscript and for their suggestions and observations.

My gratitude to Ligia Rodríguez from The College of Farmingdale at SUNY and to Eda Henao from The Borough of Manhattan Community College for their insights and letters of support.

INTRODUCTION

It has been said that long before "The Discovery" of the American continent, the Portuguese had already visited the African coasts and were involved in capturing blacks for business. Fifty years before Christopher Columbus' trip, Antonio González, a Portuguese, had captured males from the jungles of Guinea and had sold them in Lisbon, Seville and Madrid.[1] When the business expanded, the human cargo was brought to the Peninsula for distribution and "Lagos in the South of Portugal became the main slave mart."[2]

> The practice of bringing Africans as slaves to the Peninsula was initiated in 1442. Once they arrived in Spain, they became part of the household service of wealthy families. It was social prestige to own a slave. When the slave learned Spanish and embraced the Catholic religion, he/she was considered a *ladino*.[3] In order to become a *ladino* the slave had to go through a slow process of acculturation in which the African became assimilated to the culture of the metropolis.[4]

Noticing the Africans' vigor and endurance to work in the worst weather, hot or cold, the leaders of the colonies requested from Spanish King Fernando V,[5] permission to import blacks to America.[6] In 1516 the King granted a Spanish trader the authorization to import 4,000 blacks for the Spanish settlers in the

---

1. Julio Estupiñán Tello, *El negro en Esmeraldas* (Quito, Ecuador: Gráficos Nacionales, 1967): pp. 33-4. From now on as *El negro en Esmeraldas*.
2. E. D. Morel, *The Black Man's Burden. The White Man in Africa From the Fifteenth Century to World War 1* (Manchester: National Labor Press, 1920). Edited by Jim Zwick. BondocksNet.Edition, 2001. From now on as E. D. Morel.
3. Ladino: A slave who spoke the language of the master and had assimilated to the new culture.
4. Rocío Rueda Novoa, *Zambaje y Autonomía. Historia de la Gente Negra.* Siglos XVI-XVIII (Quito, Ecuador: Abaya-Yala, 2001): p. 49. From now on *as Zambaje y Autonomía.*
5. Fernando II the Catholic, Fernando V of Castile (1474-1516), King of Aragon (1479-1516). He was born in 1452 and died on September 17, 1516.
6. *El negro en Esmeraldas*, p. 34.

Indies. Afterward, the Spanish trader sold his business to a Genovese who made the importation of blacks an official enterprise and the slave trade was initiated in the American Continent.[7]

The demand for African labor grew and several European countries claimed the right to participate in the slave business. Hunting, transporting and selling blacks in American market places was the most lucrative business activity of the era; starting with the Portuguese (1442), followed by the Spaniards, the British (1562), the Dutch (1620), the French (1640), the Swedes, the Danes and the Prussians (1700s),[8] these countries benefited from the human trade.[9] African coasts were invaded by hunters in search of human game. Entire African villages were captured and thrown into the holds of slave ships.[10] In the meantime, Britain wanted to monopolize the trade and, finally, after several attempts "in 1713 the treaty of Utrecht granted to the new superpower, Britain, the right to sell slaves to the Spanish in the colonies."[11]

The idea of shipping blacks to the New World went back to the sixteenth century. It was Fray Bartolome de Las Casas (1484-1566) who first proposed that blacks should replace the Indians as forced labor; the Africans, redeemers by force, would alleviate the torture of Indians in the mitas,[12] the agricultural fields, etc. Fray De Las Casas did not realize that by replacing Indian labor with African slavery he was opening a Pandora's box. Enslaved Africans were treated worse than animals. It was believed that physical punishment was a stimulant to make them work harder. Sexual activity among blacks was induced for breeding. Their offspring were sold before they were even born.[13] De Las Casas retracted his proposal, when he saw the inhumane treatment of blacks. He finally decided that neither the Indians nor the blacks should be slaves.

---

7. Ibid.
8. E. D. Morel.
9. *El negro en Esmeraldas*, pp. 34-5, *et al.*
10. E. D. Morel.
11. Raúl Cañizares, *Cuban Santeria: Walking With the Night* (Vermont: Destiny Books): p. 128. "The Treaty of Utrecht" was an agreement between Great Britain and Spain in which British traders were granted the right to import 144,000 slaves for the colonies.
12. Mita: Forced hard labor.
13. *El negro en Esmeraldas*, pp. 35-8

However, not all Africans arrived as slaves to the New World. The first black who set foot in Esmeraldas, Ecuador,[14] was a free man. Although his name is not registered in history books, this man arrived with the conquerors of El Reyno de Quito. He came to the New World with Francisco Pizarro in 1526 and was among the thirteen who crossed the line.[15] When the Governor of Panama decided to discontinue support for Pizarro's expedition and ordered the explorers to return home, Pizarro drew a horizontal line with his sword on the sand and invited those who wanted to become rich to cross the line. He said: "To the north to be poor, to the south to be rich." The thirteen men who stepped forward are remembered as *The Thirteen of the Fame.*

On the second voyage of 1528 the expedition arrived to the coasts of what today is Colombia and the littoral of Ecuador. Before disembarking, Pizarro sent Alvaro de Molina and a Black man, who was commissioned to help the Spaniards, to explore the shore.[16] During the Conquest, numerous blacks traveled to the American continent as auxiliaries of the Conquistador. Blacks who joined the Spanish expeditions in the New World were trained in the militia.[17]

The second time Africans arrived in Ecuador they were also free. According to the *Chronicles of Esmeraldas* written by Cabello de Balboa,[18] in 1553 a Spanish vessel sailed from Panama to Peru carrying, in addition to merchandise, some blacks, males and females, to exchange for silver in Peru;[19] after the dangerous trip, the ship anchored in front of the coast of Esmeraldas with the purpose of getting food and water.

---

14. Esmeraldas is one of the twenty-two provinces of Ecuador, known as the black province and also as the green province of the country.

15. *El negro en Esmeraldas*, p. 44.

16. "El país de los Incas: Epoca de la Conquista Iberoamericana," *La Historia y sus Protagonistas.* (Ediciones Dolmen, 2001) The underlining is mine.

17. *Zambaje y Autonomía,* p. 49.

18. "Miguel Cabello de Balboa was a secular Spanish priest from Archidona, Spain. In 1556, he emigrated to Peru . . . from there he went to Quito, Ecuador . . . *The Catholic Encyclopedia,* Vol. III. Online Edition, © 2003. A. D. F. Bandelier, Transcribed by Mathew Reak. According to Federico González Suárez, "Cabello de Balboa came to the New World in 1566," *Zambaje y Autonomía,* p. 23. He "was in Esmeraldas in 1577," Norman E. Whitten Jr. *Class Kinship, and Power in an Ecuadorian Town: The Negros of San Lorenzo.* (Stanford, California: Stanford University Press, 1965): p. 23. From now on as *Class and Kinship.*

19. *Zambaje y Autonomía,* p. 23.

The Spaniards sent twenty-three blacks, seventeen males and six females, to land in search of these supplies for the ship; while waiting for their return, a strong wind threw the boat against the rocks. The scared Spaniards swam to shore trying to gather the blacks back to the ship, but they could not be found because, as soon as they reached the Ecuadorian shores, they escaped into the mountains. Confused and disoriented, the Spaniards abandoned the ship and walked along the beach toward the south; they were never seen again. With the Spaniards gone, the blacks returned to the abandoned ship and took what they needed for their survival, including weapons, and went back into the jungle. These Africans were servants of the Spaniard Alonso de Illescas from Seville, who was the owner of the ship, and were the first blacks who settled in Esmeraldas.[20]

At first, the newly arrived Africans established themselves in Pidi, a small village inhabited by the Pidi Indians. The blacks forced the Indians to recede into the mountains. When the natives tried to recuperate their land, the Africans fought back and easily defeated the Indians with firearms which[21] were unknown to the aborigines. With time, natives and blacks tolerated each other, but the latter were in charge.[22] "They recognized as a common leader a black warrior named Anton," who was called "The great wizard." [23] The acceptance of his leadership was probably due to magic arts which were very important in African culture.[24]

Under Anton, the blacks and the Pidi Indians formed an alliance to attack and invade the land of the Campace or Colorado Indian tribes from the interior of the coast.[25] When Anton died, the Africans began to fight among themselves for the leadership of the group. Black Alonso de Illescas, a ladino,[26] who was part of the group, took over the leadership. It was convenient for the group to have

---

20. *El negro en Esmeraldas*, pp. 49-50, *et al.*
21. The firearm of the era was the harquebus, which was in use in the second half of the fifteen century.
22. *El negro en Esmeraldas*, p. 50
23. *No Longer Invisible. Afro-Latin America Today.* (Ed. Minority Rights Groups. Minority Rights Publication, 1995): pp. 291-2.
24. *Zambaje y Autonomía*, p. 45.
25. *El negro en Esmeraldas*, p. 50, *et al.*
26. See footnote no. 3

Alonso as the leader because he was a ladino, the others were bozales.[27] Black Alonso was brought from Cabo Verde, Africa, to Seville when he was eight years old. He grew up in the house of Don Sebastian Alonso de Illescas. As a child he was named Enrique.[28] He adopted the full name of his master when he received the Catholic confirmation sacrament in Seville.[29] He was therefore a servant not a slave. Finally, under the command of black Alonso, the group conquered the Nigua Indians from San Miguel de Cayapa.

Alonso ruled with an iron hand the land of what today is the province of Imbabura and Pichincha,[30] until 1607, when he died of natural causes.[31] Under the blacks' rule, Africans in Esmeraldas resisted the Spaniards' attempts to conquer them. For this reason, colonization in this province took place almost a hundred years after the Spaniards were already established in other parts of the country. Other groups of blacks settled in the north coast of Manabi and, like the blacks in Esmeraldas, also resisted the Spaniards until near the end of the sixteenth century; self liberated blacks maintained their own political structure, culture and religion.

> The coastal lowlands north of Manta were conquered, not by Spaniards, but by Blacks from the Guinean Coast who, in 1570, as slaves, were shipwrecked in route from Panama to Peru. The Blacks killed or enslaved the native males and married the females. Within a generation they constituted a population of zambos[32] that resisted Spanish authority until the end of the century and afterwards managed to retain a great deal of political and cultural independence.[33]

At the turn of the seventeenth century another wreckage brought more Africans to Esmeraldas shores, further enhancing its black population. Blacks,

---

27. Bozales were the slaves either recently brought from Africa or those who did not speak the language of their masters, *Zambaje y Autonomía* p. 49.

28. Claudio Zendrón. *Cultura Negra y Espiritualidad.* (Quito: Centro Cultural Afro-Ecuatoriano, 1997): 29. From now on as *Cultura Negra y Espiritualidad.*

29. *Zambaje y Autonomía*, p. 48.

30. *El negro en Esmeraldas*, pp. 51-2.

31. *Zambaje y Autonomía*, p. 79.

32. Zambo: the offspring of the interracial marriage between African and Indian couples.

33. "Spanish Colonial Era," *U.S. Library of Congress.* Countrystudies.us/Ecuador/6.htm

mingled genetically with different indigenous ethnic groups,[34] are the basis of the origins of the predominantly black population of this province today.

Nevertheless, in addition to the cimarrones,[35] there were black slaves in Esmeraldas and in other parts of the country. The first imported Africans arrived in the Chota Valley,[36] province of Imbabura, in the late 1500s. They were acquired for breeding and for cheap labor by Jesuit Catholic priests. Based on one of Calvin's determinist theories,[37] Catholics and protestant Christians felt there wasn't anything wrong in owning slaves. Martin Luther believed that it was impossible to survive without slaves. When Indians were becoming extinct in Jesuit farms of the Chota Valley, Cacique Tulcanaza[38] brought Africans from Barbacoas, a town of the jurisdiction of Túquerres located in southern Colombia.[39] They replaced the Indians who were dying from the brutal and inhumane treatment in the mitas[40] of Chalguayaco, Carpuelas, Santiago, Cachipamba, Chamanal, Tumbabiro, Cuajara, and Pisquer. The Africans brought to Ecuador from Barbacoas were assigned to work mainly in the sugar mills.[41]

Cacique Tulcanaza was considered an outstanding representative of the Pastos aborigines who inhabited the extensive territory between the Chota River in northern Ecuador and the Guáytara River in southern Colombia. Because he knew how to read and write in Spanish, he was respected by the Spaniards and

---

34. Some ethnic groups of Esmeraldas are: the Dobe, Campace, Cayapa, Colorado, Esmeraldas, Manlaba, Nigua, Pastos, Pidi, Yumbo, etc.

35. The cimarrones were blacks who escaped from their Spanish masters. Those who escaped from their British and French masters were called maroons. Spanish *cimarrón*, English *maroon*, French *marrón*. Norman E. Whitten, Jr., and Arlene Torres. *Blackness in Latin America*, "Introduction," Vols. I and II (USA: Indiana University Press, 1998): p. 21. From now on as *Blackness in Latin America*.

36. The Chota Valley, at 1,480 meters above sea level, is located in the Andes in the northern part of Ecuador. Its population is of African origin.

37. John Calvin (1509-1564) was the second great reformer of the sixteenth century. One of his main theories was predestination: "some . . . are predestined by God to be slaves, others to be masters." *Slavery, Free Will, Revivalism. Second American Awaken*, www.piney.com/reviv/awk/html

38. The Indian Tulcanaza was the Cacique of old Tulcan the capital of the province of Carchi, at the north of Ecuador, border of Colombia. He was the first governor of Tulcan at the end of the XVI century.

39. Eduardo Martínez.*Cacique Tulcanaza* (Quito, Ecuador: Editora Andina, 1983): 49. From now on as *Tulcanaza*.

40. See footnote 12.

41. *Tulcanaza*. pp. 5, 54, 57, *et al.*

was granted some political and administrative powers. "In 1584, he went to Spain to request from the Crown some rights in favor of the Indians."[42] When the parochial church was built, and a representative of the culture of the era was needed, Cacique Tulcanaza assumed the very important mission of teaching Indians how to read, write, and also to sing, in church.[43]

Enslaved Africans arrived in Guayaquil, capital of the Guayas province and the largest city of Ecuador, in the 1630s. They came in slave ships to Panama first, then to Barbacoas, and were finally transported to Guayaquil, their final destination.[44] Other Africans also came directly from Panama and Buenaventura in the north, and from Puerto of Callao and Paita in the south. These slaves were acquired from the Spanish who had bought them from Portuguese, English and Dutch traders. The influx of blacks was very important in Guayaquil. They were considered an imported acquisition; to own a slave was a luxury and a reassurance of high economic and social status. The price paid for an African was between 400 and 500 pesos reales, a fortune at the time. Slaves' castes and nationalities were identified according to their place of origin: Angola, Arara, Bañú, Biafar, Carabalí, Congo, Malemba, Mandinga, Mozambique, Naluque, etc. The Africans born in the New World (black creoles) were also identified according to their place of birth; for example, black creoles from Quito, from Guayaquil, from Panamá, etc. There was also a denomination for free blacks depending on how their freedom was obtained. If their freedom was bought on installments, similar to what is today a savings certificate, the free black was identified as "negro horro" or "negra horra."[45]

A letter of "horro" was a document stating the wish of the master to grant freedom to the slave, who was identified by name, when the master did not have enough money to buy the certificate of freedom. The letter of "horro" was signed

---

42. Ibid.
43. Ibid, p. 48.
44. Ezio Garay Arellano. *Varios Escritos Históricos de Guayaquil y su Provincia* (Guayaquil: Archivo Histórico del Guayas, 1999): p. 49. From now on as Ezio Garay Arellano.
45. Ezio Garay Arellano, p. 57.

8

before a notary and the Royal Treasurer, who represented the Crown.[46] Newly free blacks formed groups and chose the outskirts of Guayaquil as living quarters. Today, there are blacks everywhere in the city, but there are also neighborhoods with concentrations of black residents. In these barrios, blacks keep aspects of their culture alive through religious practices, feasts, musical festivals, myths and legends.

In the province of Loja, southern Ecuador, on the border with the Amazonian region, there was a huge black population, some were Cimarrones,[47] others slaves. The slaves who arrived in Loja were put to work mainly in households as domestics or in gold mines. Many escaped from the mines and engaged in agricultural work in other regions. In 1557, when Don Juan Salinas de Loyola[48] attempted to conquer the Jívaros,[49] he took some blacks slaves with him for help. In 1579 during the Jívaro upraising there probably were self liberated blacks and mestizos among the insurgents.[50]

During the colonial era blacks spread to other parts of the Loja province. In Loja city, the capital, there was at one time a black neighborhood with a concentration of African residents. Presently, one can hardly find blacks in Loja. It seems they left the region, intermingled with the native population or were somehow absorbed into the general population. Today, there are no individuals that can be identified as blacks in Loja.[51]

---

46. Ibid.

47. See footnote 35.

48. Juan Salinas de Loyola, Spanish Conqueror of the beginnings of the Conquest and Colonization of the Indies. He established the exploitation of the mines of Cañar from 1534-1563.

49. Jívaro is a generic name for four tribes, the Ashuar, Aguaruna, Huambisa and Shuar. They inhabit the Ecuadorian and Peruvian Amazon region. The Shuar are famous for their head hunting and head shrinking skills. They reduce the head of an enemy to a size of a fist and display the shrunken head as a trophy. "Shrunken Heads," *monstrous.com*, 1999-2003.

50. Norman E. Whitten, Jr., and Diego Quiroga, "To Rescue National Dignity. Blackness as a Quality of Nationalist Creativity in Ecuador," *Blackness in Latin America* Vol. I., pp. 82-3.

51. Ibid.

Because of similarities with the African climate, the Esmeraldas province was alluring to blacks. In 1830, when Ecuador became a Republic[52] there was a strong black emigration from neighboring Colombia. They came on their own to Esmeraldas attracted by the rubber, tagua,[53] cascarilla,[54] palo de balsa,[55] and banana industries. They established themselves in the country and married Ecuadorian mulattoes. In 1852 when slavery was abolished in Ecuador,[56] liberated slaves from the Chota province came down to Esmeraldas, especially those from the Jesuit black breeding grounds.

Jesuits exploited the slave trade from 1585 until their expulsion in 1767.[57] Although slavery officially ended in 1852, there were slaves until the late nineteenth century. Today, Indians and blacks share cultures as evidenced by their food, clothing, dance, music, etc. It is common to see a black playing an Indian rondador[58] and an Indian playing an African drum. Black intermarriage with Indians created a new race, the zambo.[59] Today, very few families in Esmeraldas could claim to be "white." Estupiñán Tello, the author of *El negro en*

---

52. Ecuador earned independence from Spain in 1822 and formed part of The Great Colombia (1822-1830). The Great Colombia included Colombia, Venezuela, Ecuador and Panama. In 1830 Ecuador left The Great Colombia and became a separate country.

53. The cadi palm tree produces de tagua, a vegetal ivory. Cadi leaves are used to cover roofs of country houses. *El habla del Ecuador, Diccionario de Ecuatorianismos* (Quito: Universidad del Azuay, 1992): 187

54. Cascarilla: A yellowish bitter, aromatic medicinal substance extracted from the bark of an Indigenous American "euforbiácea" tree. DRAE, XXI Edition, Madrid, 1992. The Indians use cascarilla powder to clean their teeth.

55. Palo de balsa: Light, white wood.

56. Slavery was abolished in Ecuador on September 25, 1852 under President, General Jose Maria Urvina (1852-1856), although slavery persisted in some parts of Ecuador until the late nineteenth century. The initiative for the abolition of slavery came from England example; Simon Bolivar and Lincoln followed. Anti-abolitionists opposed the manumission of slaves because they believed that without black labor there would be no bread, sugar, cotton, ships, clothing and exploitation of mines. That is to say that white men would die of starvation. *El negro en la historia: Raíces Africanas en la Nacionalidad Ecuatoriana. -500 años-* (Quito, Ecuador: Centro Cultural Afroecuatoriano, 1992): p. 184.

57. Gary Smith, *The History of the Catholic Church in Latin America and Liberation Theology* (1982), Vol. V, (Yale, New Haven: Teachers Institute, © 2005).

58. Rondador: Indigenous wind musical instrument similar to the Spanish zampoña. The rondador is a double row panpipes made of several bamboo tubes of different sizes tied together.

59. See footnote 32.

Esmeraldas said: "In general, we all, to a greater or lesser degree, have black roots."[60]

The influx of blacks to Ecuador continued until the late nineteenth and the early twentieth centuries. During Eloy Alfaro's era, four thousand blacks came from Jamaica to work in the construction of the Andean railroad.[61] When the work ended, some went back to Jamaica, others went to Esmeraldas. They did not stay in the region because they could not adapt to the weather conditions of the Andes. "The implacable climate, the snake bites, illnesses, and fever produced by the sting of mosquitoes, took the life of dozens of workers that resulted in the escape of others."[62]

The history of blacks in Ecuador is long and painful not only because, as slaves, they were subjected to all kinds of abuses, but because of the social oppression they have endured in freedom. While Indians have been the main target of discrimination because they have been considered inferior to whites and white-mestizos,[63] blacks have been victims of racism simply by being ignored. Indians are considered "our Indian problem" because they are the most deprived, but the situation of blacks is hardly mentioned. Ecuadorians of African ancestry are not considered a social predicament because they are not recognized as part of the national chemistry, neither are they part of the national "mestizo."[64]

"The Afro-Ecuadorian has a history before [and after] his arrival to the New World, but [this history] is not included in school textbooks."[65] Blacks'

---

60. *El negro en Esmeraldas*, p. 85

61. Eloy Alfaro took power in 1895. He amended the Constitution and in 1897 was elected president for a four year period until 1901. He was elected again in 1906-1911. In 1912 he returned from Europe with the intent of pursuing another presidential term. He was imprisoned on arrival and in January 1912 a group of his opponents invaded the prison and he was lynched by the mob. Julio Estupiñán Tello, *Esmeraldas de ayer* (Esmeraldas, Ecuador: REDIGRAF): p. 125. From now on as *Esmeraldas de ayer*.

62. *Quito Distrito Metropolitano Railroad of Ecuador.* www.quito.gov.ec/ingles/inrailroad.htm

63. "People classified as *mestizo*, (Indian-Spanish mixed) usually refer to themselves as *blanco* (white)." *Blackness in Latin America*, Vol. I, pp. 13-14, *et al.*

64. Jean Rahier. "Mami, ¿qué será lo que quiere el negro?" Representaciones racistas en la *Revista Vistazo*, 1957-1991. Yachana.org/ecuatorianistas/essays/essays.html. From now on as Jean Rahier.

65. Wistting Fierro Ruiz, *Los Ecuatorianos Despreciados y Humillados* (Cuenca: Publicaciones y Papeles, 1973): p. 44.

input in shaping the country has not been recognized. African participation in the wars of independence from Spain is not mentioned in any elementary or high school textbooks. Class lectures and readings have centered on the arrival of the Spaniards and their encounter with the natives. We grew up learning that Spaniards born on the American continent,[66] with the help of the mestizos[67] were the ones who fought the wars of independence. The ethnicity of Simón Bolívar, who considered himself a mulatto, and was held in contempt by "pure blooded" Spaniards,[68] was never mentioned in Ecuadorian history classes.[69] Ignoring the presence of blacks in Ecuador persists until today. Usually census reports indicate Ecuadorian ethnicity as 65% mestizo (mixed Indian-Spanish), 25% Indian, 7% Spanish and 3% black. There are no percentage records of the overwhelming mulatto and zambo population of the country.[70] A 2004 census registers: "Approximately 90% of the population of Ecuador is composed of Native Americans and mestizos (people of mixed Native American and European ancestry), the remainder equally divided between Europeans (chiefly of Spanish descent) and blacks."[71]

Anthropological studies show that Ecuador racial and economic problems involve Indians, not blacks, and the theory of "blanqueamiento" (whitening) which enforces "race improvement" also applies only to Indians, not to blacks. Ecuadorian texts written by whites and white mestizos refer to blacks as "the relegated others." References concerning blacks are scarce and very brief because

---

66. Criollos: Spaniards born in America who resented the Spaniards born in Spain because the latter held the best positions and looked down on their Spanish-American counterparts.

67. See footnote 63.

68. "Spaniard themselves have a strong African heritage, the result of being next to North Africa and receiving African culture over the millennia, including the eight centuries the Moors occupied Southern Spain, from 710AD to 1492 AD. This gives rise to a famous quote from Simon Bolivar: *We are no longer Europeans just as Spain is no longer European, because of its African blood, character and institutions*," AfroCubaWeb,sa, 2003.

69. "In literary and historical treatises on Simon Bolivar, his possible black ancestry as evidenced by his "mulatto blood" is mentioned from time to time," "The Black Americas and the African Diaspora" in *Blackness in Latin America*, Vol. I, p. 11.

70. Http://www.infoplease.com/ipa/A0107479.html

71. *Encarta*, Online Encyclopedia, 2004, 1997-2004.

12

they are not considered part of the population that needs to be civilized as the Indians are.[72]

Yet, African heritage in Ecuadorian culture, language and religion is alive all over the country, especially in black towns such as Atacame, Camarones, Chota, Esmeraldas, La Toma, Limones, Muisne, Osteones, Rio Verde, Rocafuerte, San Lorenzo, San Mateo, the Chota valley, to name just a few.

People from African extraction in the Chota Valley have blended African, European and Indian elements in their way of life and culture. For example, the "Bomba" is a typical black dance from the mountains of Minda and the Chota.[73] It is played with African drums, rhythmical Indian instruments and Spanish guitars. The "bottle dance" includes a bottle balanced on the head of the dancer; this dance artistically depicts the African tradition of carrying water and other goods on top of the head rather than on the back, like the Indians do. Elderly Chota women wear traditional African style outfits. The official language in the Chota Valley is Spanish, but African words and syntax remain blended in the Spanish spoken in this region.[74]

In Esmeraldas the essence of African cultures and religions are part of daily life. Folk healers practice all over the country, especially in the northern coast of the province of Esmeraldas where the cimarrones brought the healing practices of the African "sobador" and "curandero." The "sobador" is a chiropractor. He corrects all kinds of dislocations, fractures and sprains. He is a keen healer who can distinguish a dislocation from a fracture. He can heal people as well as animals."[75] The "curandero" is a herbalist. He heals in the name of God, Jesus and Mary. Using herb concoctions, he is quite successful with snake bites, etc."[76] "Brujos" and "guardaespaldas" come to Esmeraldas from time to time to remove spells from malign sources. The "brujos" are active sorcerers and

72. Jean Rahier

73. Adalberto Ortiz. *Poetas del Ecuador* (Quito: Casa de la Cultura Ecuatoriana): p. 119.

74. *Class and Kinship*, p. 80.

75. Ibid, pp. 79-80.

76. Ibid, pp. 79-81.

witch hunters. The "guardaespaldas" protects the brujo from rebounding spells or from the spells from other brujos.[77]

In Afro-Ecuadorian cosmology, spirits inhabit nature. They dwell in trees, rivers, swamps and seas; these entities play an important role in the spirituality of Esmeraldas. "African deities dwell in another dimension, from which they alternatively protect and harm their people. Afro-Ecuadorians from Esmeraldas honor them."[78] In villages where people believe in legends and folk tales, the deities materialize at will.

History and myth blend to nourish Afro-Ecuadorian tales. For example, according to legend, the spiritual entities of the swamps are the product of a love relationship between the devil and a black woman. They met in the seventh century when a slave ship capsized near the Esmeraldas shores. As in real life, the blacks of the legend set themselves free, killed their captors and established themselves as a free community. The aborigines fought for their land, and a fierce battle between blacks and Indians began. The screams reached the depth of hell and the devil heard the moaning of the wounded. He came to Esmeraldas with the intention of exterminating the Indians and the blacks because he hated both races. The devil arrived in the shape of the black Prince, Macumba, and with his black arts helped the blacks to win the battle. But the devil that arrived with the intention of killing and destroying was defeated by love, a beautiful black princess who turned him into a peaceful family man. From this union la Gualgura y la Tunda were born. They form part of the numerous entities that shape the black mythology of Esmeraldas.

Some of the well known entities of Esmeraldas folk tales are: El Barco Fantasma, El Barrero, El Bombero, La Bruja, El Cuco, El Diablo, El Duende, Los Fuegos Fatuos, La Gualcara, La Gualgura, El Marinero, La Mondongada, La Mula, El Riviel, La Sirena, El Tin Tin, La Tunda, La Viuda.[79]

77. Ibid, pp. 80-1.
78. Dora Quintero, *Los espíritus del más allá. Diez personajes de la mitología Afroesmeraldeña* (Quito: Abya-Yala, 1999): p. 7. From now on as *Los espíritus del más allá.*
79. Julio Estupiñán Tello, *Esmeraldas de Ayer* (Quito: REDIGRAF, 1996): pp. 80-4. From now on as *Esmeraldas de Ayer.*

Barco Fantasma is a ghost ship that appears on odd occasions, usually at night. It anchors near the shore where a person devoted to the devil lives. The ghost ship is a steam vessel of souls who belong to the devil. People who have not obeyed God's laws must constantly follow the ghost ship. Those who are baptized and obey God's laws do not fear the ghost ship.[80]

Barrero protects the animals from the jungle and punishes hunters who hurt and abandon a wounded animal.[81] The Bombero is a man who plays a bombo.[82]

Bruja is a witch who, in order to obtain knowledge and supernatural powers, worships the devil. She performs rituals in secret with evil intentions.[83] She sucks the blood of newborn babies. To keep her away from a newborn baby a cross must be placed at the head of the bed; an open scissor simulating the cross also keeps the witch away from the cradle. The witch can turn herself into a bird and is able to fly. [84]

Cuco is the boogey man used in pedagogy to teach children to behave, or he will take them away.[85]

Diablo is the devil who builds friendships with people greedy for money. People who make a pact with the "diablo" get rich very quickly, but in exchange must render their souls to him.

One tale about the devil tells how he arrived in a village disguised as a respectful man. It was hot and humid and an intangible heat was embedded in the environment. It seemed as if steam penetrated the thighs of transients who, perspiring heavily, traveled in narrow canoes toward the North of the Cayapa River. When a loud whistle was heard from the shore, people turned their heads toward the big trees where an enormous parrot, flapping its wings, warned in a

---

80. *Cultura negra y espiritualidad*, p. 112
81. Ibid, p. 113.
82. Bombo: a kind of drum, *El Habla del Ecuador. Diccionario de Ecuatorianismos* (Quito: Universidad del Azuay, 1992): p. 187. The dictionaries consulted do not register any information about the Bombero as a spiritual entity.
83. Ibid.
84. Martha Escobar Konanz, *La frontera Imprecisa* (Quito: Centro Cultural Afroecuatoriano, 1990): p. 35. From now on as *La frontera imprecisa*. Esmeraldas de Ayer, p. 61.
85. *Cultura negra y espiritualidad*, p. 113.

shrieking voice: "The devil makes friends with poor businessmen, who become inexplicably rich after they encounter him."

Remberto Angulo, who, just few months before did not have a cent, became inexplicably rich. People envied him. He drank rum with the foreigner who had arrived in town from nowhere. They stayed out drinking past midnight until the wee hours of the morning.

Remberto Angulo neither attended mass, nor complied with the precepts of the Catholic Church. One day he gave a big party in which the guest of honor was the good looking foreigner. The visitor was dressed in blue pants, red shirt and a big hat and stayed near the band. The owner of the house ordered: "Good Heavens! Play a berejú,[86] we want to dance!" The band played the berejú and the handsome visitor began to dance wildly, with gestures and movements that made women incontinent. From time to time, he stopped dancing and approached the band to take the place of the musician who played the tiple.[87] Black women with strong legs and bare feet also began dancing. Full of pleasure, they contorted their bodies until they were exhausted. All the people at the party began to drink heavily and jumped up and down, while in the distance, one could hear a resounding laugh and a tune saying: "Move your hips my berejú. Wow my berejú. The devil is nearby, my berejú. Wow my berejú . . ."[88]

At about midnight, Remberto Angulo's son woke up to the noise. He went to the living room and saw that the man who was stumping on the floor with fury had a rooster's crest and goat feet. He also noticed that the house was sinking at every foot stamping of the man who at the same time was singing at the top of his voice. "Tum-ba que tum-ba, el tum del Diablo va retum-bando.!" [89]

— "Mom, mom!," Arcadio screamed anxious to warn his mother of what was going on. But because she was drunk, she kept dancing in circles, contorting

---

86. Verejú or berejú: Original word from one of the Bantu languages, meaning Demon. Adalberto Ortiz, *Juyungo* (Quito: Editorial Casa de la Cultura Ecuatoriana, 1957): p. 317.

87. A twelve stringed treble guitar.

88. *Los espíritus del más allá*, pp. 41-7.

89. "Sink, sink at the rhythm of the devil's tune."

her hips with lust and perspiring heavily, without paying attention to what her son was trying to tell her. The boy insisted:

— "Mom, the foreigner has a rooster's crest and goat feet!"

Since his mother paid no attention to him, the boy went to look for his grandfather who lived nearby and brought him to the party. The elderly man saw the people dancing in a frenzy as if they were under a spell while the foreigner repeated the following tune: "Angelina is in the room, my brothers in the beyond, come all my friends come, we are taking them all."

The old man paid close attention to the lyrics of the tune the foreigner was singing and keeping the same rhythm responded with deep emotion: "I come from far from beyond. I have a headache, because I do not want to mention the Magnificent, the Great . . ." When the grandfather finished that phrase, the sinking house immediately resurfaced and the foreigner, converted into a tiger, vanished.[90]

Duende appears as extremely short man wearing a huge hat, smoking a cigar and playing a guitar. He is a charming spiritual entity, very friendly, playful, and a womanizer, always in pursuit of young girls. He throws flowers, coins and other things to them. He appears in the barn at night to harass the horses. He likes to ride on each horse's neck and holds himself tight from the horsehair, as if it were the reins. He forces the animals to run around the stable until they are exhausted. In the morning the horses appear very tired with tangled horsehair, in total disarray.[91] Duende is a fallen angel who was cast out of heaven. That is why he has a gift for music and knows how to play the guitar. He can teach prayers that protect one from imminent danger.

He pursues pubescent young girls who have not had any sexual experience as their breasts are developing. He does not cause any physical injury to them, he just wants to touch their breasts.[92]

---

90. *Los espíritus del más allá*, pp. 41-7.
91. *Esmeraldas de ayer*, pp. 82-4.
92. *Cultura negra y espiritualidad*, pp. 111-12.

Fuegos Fatuos are "small flames carried by the animas to show where there are buried treasures."[93] These flames usually appear at night to tempt rural men into making a pact with the devil.

Gualcara, a variation of Gualgura, is a baby black chick or, in another version, a black hen, with recently hatched chicks. It appears in the afternoon or at night "crying" around the house. When someone tries to help, it leads the person to the woods until he/she gets lost. Gualcara is the transformation of Tunda and its story is unknown.[94]

Gualgura, is a demonic spirit that appears in the shape of a harmless black hen with baby chickens. It attracts its victims to far away places until they get lost.[95] Gualgura, an offspring of Tunda and the devil, also appears as an overgrown chicken with ruffled feathers, and an enormous aggressively open beak. She cries at night, in the backyard of country houses, imitating a lost baby chicken. Parents send their children to help the creature, and then Gualgura attracts them to faraway places where Tunda is waiting.[96]

Mondongada appears first, looking like a fairly big mushroom spread at ground level; it gives off a glowing pale light and slowly engulfs its victims until it suffocates them.[97]

Mula is a mule that usually appears at night on Fridays. Her presence is noticed because of the clinking noise of the bell that hangs from her neck. Mula is a woman who is transformed into a mule as punishment for having sexual relations with a Catholic priest. She recovers her human form during the day.[98]

There are several tales about a mule. For example, there was once a widow who became pregnant and because the town suspected she had a sexual relationship with the priest, she was called Mula.[99]

---

93. Adalberto Ortiz, *La Entundada* (Quito: Casa de la Cultura Ecuatoriana, 1971): p. 117. From now on as *La entundada*.

94. *Cultura negra y espiritualidad*, p. 112.

95. *Esmeraldas de ayer*, pp. 82-4, *et al.*

96. Ibid.

97. Ibid.

98. *La Entundada*, pp. 93-5.

99. Ibid, p. 95.

Riviel is a restless spirit. Dweller of estuaries, canals, seas, and roads, he appears dressed in black, riding on one end of a mutilated canoe where he carries an oil lamp. He covers his skull with a scarf, and materializes in different parts of the canoe to confuse and terrorize his victims. He haunts those who travel the rivers at night. When travelers naively ask him for light for their cigars, he shows them his skull. The traveler sometimes capsizes or waits for daylight shaking with hypothermia. If Riviel appears on land, he follows the victim zigzagging to drive him insane. With new technology and transportation the image of Riviel is slowly disappearing from the mythology of Esmeraldas.[100]

Riviel is the soul of a drowned man whose body was never retrieved from the river and therefore was never buried. For this reason, he is looking for someone who can rescue his bones from the bottom of the river. Sometimes he is invisible, he can only be perceived as a light sailing toward the estuary of the river.[101] This legend about Riviel comes from people's preoccupation with the drowned and the conviction that their souls cannot be saved until their bodies are buried.[102]

Sirena is a mermaid. She dwells in the water and appears at sea combing her hair with a comb made of gold. She sings to allure seamen to the bottom of the sea[103] where she lives. Another version of Sirena defines her as a vision or enchantress from the water, the rocks, and the caves. According to Antonio Corozo, a folk healer, the place where Sirena lives is an enchanted location. In the San Lorenzo Pailon[104] one could hear Sirena's melody sounding like a marimba and other kinds of music, just like songs played in the radio, and like a rooster singing at the bottom of the sea. Sirena allures the chosen man to her enchanted world and makes him her mate.

Her particular shape, half woman, half fish, white and blond catches the man's eye. Several men have seen her in the estuary of the Cayapa river, in castle

---

100. *Esmeraldas de ayer*, pp. 84-5, *et al.*
101. *Cultura negra y espiritualidad*, p. 112.
102. Ibid.
103. *Los espíritus del más allá*, pp. 9-16.
104. Pailón: dell, valley.

towers, the Pailón of San Lorenzo, etc., but no one has gone down to her enchanted world because when she asks her usual question: "Whom do you fall in love with, with the woman or with her comb?" All men answer her: "With the comb!" When Sirena hears this response, she gets mad, disappears and the enchantment ends.[105]

Tin Tin is another name for Duende. Tin Tin appears to young women who have long black hair and big eyes with long curled eyelashes. Tin Tin is very clean and neat. In order to get rid of him the victim must sit on the toilet and pretend she is eating while defecating. He will be disgusted and the girl will never see him again.

Tunda is a spirit of the swamps. She appears as a homely deformed black woman with a big lower lip and with one leg like a "molinillo,"[106] (whiskbroom). She is sterile. To make up for barrenness, she kidnaps black children, especially those who disobey their parents; Tunda takes the victims to her cave where she turns the captive kids into Tundas like herself.[107]

In another version, Tunda had a son. She killed him and God condemned her to wander the earth for eternity and to give birth to deformed children. She has one leg like whiskbroom and the other one like a beast, ending in a cloven hoof.[108] She makes children dizzy with her stench and takes them to the high slopes of a mountain, undresses them and rubs a foul jelly-like substance on their skin. With her evil powers, she makes children forget their parents and siblings, forcing them to follow her unconditionally. She feeds raw shrimp to her captives.[109]

Sometimes Tunda takes the appearance of a woman known to the victim. She can also look like a man. It is believed that she has no sexual definition. More often, she assumes the appearance of the mother of the child she wants to kidnap, takes him to her home, and, with fumes coming from her mouth, makes

---

105. *El negro en la historia*, p. 90.
106. Molinillo: A rustic old fashion kitchen utensil made of wood. It is used to beat hot chocolate, home made butter, etc.
107. *Esmeraldas de ayer*, pp. 82-4.
108. Ibid.
109. Ibid.

the child lose his mind. She teaches him how to dance and turns him into her lover.[110]

During the child's wake, the relatives must beat a drum very loudly to keep Tunda away. She is eager for children's cadavers, she must therefore be kept away. It is also believed that Tunda kidnaps adult males. In order to rescue a victim from Tunda, a large group of people must go to where Tunda lives with a drum, a rifle and gun powder. The noises from the drum and the shotgun scare off Tunda and she escapes leaving the victim behind. Tunda also stays away from anything sacred, such as prayers, holy water, scapulars, etc. She is also scared of whips. For example, one day Tunda was going to kidnap a child who showed her the whip, and she left.[111] Tunda is hardly seen today, but it is believed that she lives in the heart of the woods. Once in a while one can find her whiskbroom footprints next to a peel of a raw shrimp.

Viuda is a widow that appears at night to drunkards and womanizers. She takes the appearance of a beautiful woman dressed in black who wanders around cemeteries where she lures her victims and kills them. This myth emphasizes the aura of the cemetery, a place no one approaches at night. Viuda also safeguards the honor of married and engaged women because decent women do not go out late at night. Therefore, in order to avoid Viuda, the womanizer has no other choice than to stop his sexual endeavors. Viuda myth has a concrete moral message for womanizers.[112] Viuda can also appear in places other than the cemetery. She also dresses according to the occasion. For example, Héctor Horacio, a womanizer and trasnochador,[113] arrived at the shore looking for an affair. He scoped the beach interested in every woman who passed him by. He was impressed by the beauty of a petite woman who was standing by a deck. She also looked at him and made a sign asking him to come near her. She was young, elegant, beautiful and was wearing an unusual perfume. The woman was pale and

---

110. *Cultura negra y espiritualidad*, p. 111.

111. Laura Hidalgo alzadora, *Décimas esmeraldeñas* (Quito: Serial Artes Gráficas, Banco Central del Ecuador, 1982): p. 78.

112. *Cultura negra y espiritualidad.*, pp. 112-13

113. Trasnochador: A man who likes to stay out all night drinking and having fun until the wee hours of the morning.

her complexion was as soft as tissue paper. "She is the most adorable creature I have ever seen," Héctor thought.

Alluring in her red tight dress, she slowly approached him. When he felt her breath, he wanted to melt inside her. They spent the day on the beach. When the light began to fade, he accepted her invitation for a cup of coffee in her apartment. When they arrived at her apartment, the woman went straight to the bedroom and emerged from it smiling and wearing a see-through nightgown. After the cup of coffee the passion between them reached the highest level of pleasure. They caressed each other and made love. At midnight, she asked him to leave. Early in the morning the next day, as soon as he woke up,

Horacio remembered her. He was jubilant and a strong desire to see her again dominated him. But when he arrived at her house, he was very disappointed. He was surprised to see that the house where he spent the night was surrounded by a somber fence. What could have happened? The place was surrounded with the silence of death. He called her, but no one answered. After few seconds and because of his screams calling for her, a peasant woman came to find out what was going on. After explaining to the peasant woman the reason why he came to the place, she answered:

— It is very strange! It was so long ago!

— Why? I met her yesterday and I want to see her again! He said.

— I believe you have not seen her at all because she died several years ago.

He felt a cold sweat running down his spine. However, he wanted to see the place inside. In fact, under the dim light he could see the house was totally empty. There were only two cups of coffee on an old ragged table. Since that day, Héctor Horacio sits on a bench, with wondering eyes, foaming from his mouth like an idiot.[114]

In another version, Viuda arrives to the shore in a canoe. One can hear the noise of the oars as the canoe approaches. She leaves from the canoe and walks on the deck. She is well dressed, elegant, wearing a nice hat, holding an umbrella

---

114. *Los espíritus del más allá*, pp. 55-6.

and wearing perfume. One can hear her steps attracting the womanizer with a magnetic force. Viuda takes men to the cemetery where she eats them and discards their bones. If she does not eat them, she turns them into sleepwalkers. The victims will be in a sleepwalking state for ever.[115]

Africans are very spiritual people. Afro-Ecuadorian myths and legends are inspired by a strong belief in the interaction between this life and the life after death. Every Afro-Ecuadorian town has its own religious practices and beliefs which deeply influence their lives. Since traditional African faiths are at the core of the actions of every African, there is not a distinct separation between the sacred and the secular.[116] Therefore, the black mythology of Ecuador is strongly related to African's religious beliefs, and spiritual entities play an important role in Afro-Ecuadorian teaching and learning moral codes through in every step of life.

African cultures, values and religions prevail not only in the officially recognized black towns of Ecuador, but all over the country. Although statistics reduce black presence in Ecuador to a minimum 3% of the total population, the truth is that African heritage is alive in the overwhelming majority of Ecuadorian zambos and mulattos who are defined as "mestizos."

Niza Fabre

---

115. *La frontera imprecise*, p. 35.
116. Ibid, p. 264, footnote 125.

CHAPTER 1

HISTORY OF THE GARIFUNA

The Garifuna ethnicity consists of two racial groups: Carib-Indian and black. The Garifuna is a homogeneous group, despite the small differences of the group in each region, with a population of approximately 75 to 80 thousand. They live in fifty three towns along the Atlantic coast of Honduras, Guatemala and Belize. Another group lives near Laguna de Las Perlas in Nicaragua (cfr. Davidson, pp. 15-25).

Throughout their history, the Garifunas have maintained a deeply rooted tradition of unending struggles for freedom, expressed through a series of wars against internal forces, such as rival tribes, or against external forces, such as the British or the French empires. In spite of the odds, the Garifunas have kept their culture, values, language, and life style intact. It is extraordinary to see how in villages, established along the Atlantic coast, the Garifuna share common characteristics, such as friendship ties, family and social history which strengthen their hidden alliance, even though they are spread among four nations.

The origins of the Garifunas take us at least 1,500 years back to the Cuenca of the Orinoco, to the North West of South America where two main Indian groups, the Amarillo Caribs and the Arawaks lived. They used to survive by hunting, fishing, fruit gathering, and agriculture. "Probably the elaboration of the traditional cassava, staple food of the Garifuna, may have been developed in that zone. Some of the instruments used by the Amerindians living there today are the same ones used by Garifunas" (cfr. Roy S.: I). Also, it is possible that the skills used in handling their canoes were acquired on rivers and ocean beaches. Probably, due to the population growth and to the rivalry between the two groups

(Caribs and Arawaks) the latter began the exodus around the year 1400, but the Caribs, their bitter enemies, followed them step by step through the lesser Antilles, Puerto Rico, Española, Cuba and Jamaica. The Caribs constantly harassed Puerto Rico up until the arrival of Christopher Columbus, and it seems that the presence of Christopher Columbus was one of the reasons that prevented them from self organization and defense.

Roy Sebastian maintains that: "Caribs diminished the number of Arawak men and took their women. As a result of this union Carib language incorporated several Arawak words; in addition, several expressions have remained, including one for men from (Carib) and another word for women from (Arawak). Still today there are traces of masculine and feminine expressions found in Garifuna language. For example, the masculine pronoun "I" is "au," while the feminine pronoun is "nguna." Otto Stoll in his work "Etnología de Guatemala" (pp. 35-43), contradicts this theory. He bases his argument on the impossibility of agreeing with the description of Rochefort in *Histoire naturelle et morale des Iles Antilles* published in Rotterdam in 1681, about pure Caribs, Amarillos, or Arawaks and applies it to the Caribs of Honduras and Guatemala of today. Otto Stoll continues: "I want to point out that the observation made by Rochefort, that the language of insular women was in certain ways similar to the language of Continental Arawaks, can be refuted just by consulting any vocabulary taken from books mentioned at the beginning of this chapter."[1]

There is a long list of words used by Castilian men, and Carib women, and a third list of words used by Arawaks of South America. Comparing the four pronunciations, Otto Stoll concludes:

> In the short list of words that I give above, there is only one word, 'Caxi,' meaning 'sun' in the language spoken by Carib women, that resembles the Arawak diction 'caxei' which means 'moon;' from this we can assume that the statement cannot be applied to the Caribs of Santo Domingo, about whom I referred before, and to verify the existing difference between the idiom of Carib men and women one should look for another reason (Otto Stoll, p. 41).

---

1. Otto Stoll, *Etnología de Guatemala*. From now on as Otto Stoll.

Caribs and Arawaks once had a very good relationship with the Spanish conqueror, but they soon found out the true intentions of the latter, which were to exploit their rich resources and use them as slaves or as cheap labor. Therefore, they had no other option than to defend themselves and struggle for the sake of their own survival. The Arawaks, who were much more peaceful people than their counterparts, were easily subdued and very quickly eliminated by the Spaniards. Meanwhile the Caribs, who had a social structure based on a strong military system, defended themselves with tenacity.[2] During the entire sixteenth century, the Caribs harassed the Spanish settlers who had invaded their land, and sometimes the Caribs also took black slaves from the Spanish (cfr. Renard, quot. *RGAC*, 25).

According to Taylor's description, quoted by La Solien (p. 43 ss), blacks had established themselves in Saint Vincent by 1625. On the other hand, the Dominic Armand de la Paix referred to the presence of some blacks brought in by two Spanish ships which capsized around 1635. The truth was that blacks took the ships, killed their masters, and headed to the Island where they sought refuge. Armand de la Paix continues: In the year 1646, some blacks from Saint Vincent who were in Saint Lucia Island killed several French men from Martinique who were in transit on the Island. These killings angered the Caribs from Dominica because they were afraid of retaliation (cfr. *RGAC*, 29). It is also said that the Catholic missionaries were present in Saint Vincent Island in 1635. Since then, one can trace the following chronology.

Chronology

1660: French, English, and Indian chiefs in Basse Terre (Guadalupe) signed a treaty in which European powers agreed not to interfere with Red and Black Caribs' affairs, assuring their perpetual possession of Dominica and Saint

---

2. There are examples of Carib men who threw themselves into ravines killing themselves rather than being subdued into slavery and inhuman treatment. The struggle to maintain their freedom was long and fierce (Roy Sebastian I). From the XVI to the XVII centuries the relationship between black Carib and black escapees from the lesser Antilles became strong. At first, they rejected each other, but later they developed an alliance to attack the copper colored Indians (perhaps the Amarillo or Arawak Indians).

Vincent Islands. In return, the Caribs agreed not to attack the Europeans, (*S.* 43; *RGAC*, 27, and 29).

1667: Saint Vincent Island was inhabited by Indians and blacks who escaped from ships and from neighboring islands such as Barbados (*S.* 43).

1668: Dominica and Saint Vincent Islands came under English power by force. Among other things, the Caribs agreed to send back the fugitive slaves who had escaped from the English possessions (*RGAC*, 26-7).

1675: A Portuguese ship capsized near Saint Vincent. According to a legend, however, it did not capsize but was diverted by the slaves on board the ship who then liberated themselves (*R.*, 29).

1676: According to a document cited by Roy Sebastian, there were around 3,000 blacks in Saint Vincent, but it is not clear if the reference is about slaves or fugitives and their Black or Red Carib descendants.

1683: According to the reference given by Sieur La Borde, (cfr. *S.* 44) the English attacked Martinique and Saint Vincent, killing and destroying everything in their way.

1685: The treaty between the British and all the chiefs from Saint Vincent and Saint Lucia was concluded (*R.* 31). According to Governor Stapleton, there were 600 blacks in Saint Vincent. Later on, Colonel Philip Werner spoke of 3,000 blacks (*R.* 28). It was a fact that the black community increased, thanks to fugitives from Barbados and other Islands; it grew so much that it surpassed the Indian population in the last decade of the seventeenth century. "Blacks obliged the Indians to retreat towards the Sotavento side of the Island, saving for themselves the most pleasant and fertile side toward Barlovento" (*R.* 31).

1700: When Jean-Baptiste Labat visited the Island, he noticed that the blacks had become very powerful and that the Caribs were distrustful, but they did not interfere with the interracial mixture of the various groups, (*S.* 44). The struggle for freedom was hard and constant throughout the eighteenth century. The colonizers felt uncomfortable with the presence of the Black Carib group which was well armed and experienced in guerilla tactics. This was considered a threat to the slave system and to the security of the whites (*R.* 31).

1719: The Governor of Martinique acknowledged the colonizers' complaint and sent his French troops with 500 soldiers who, with the help from the Carib Indians, defeated the Black Caribs. They set villages on fire and destroyed plantations, but the Blacks Caribs could not be captured; they sought refuge in the mountains where the same Carib Indians refused to persecute them. From their refuge the Black Caribs harassed the French so much that the latter got tired of these war like tactics and achieved peace through diplomatic approaches (*S.* 45 and *R.* 31-32).

1725: The English tried to take over the Island, but the black chief "who spoke excellent French, answered with the formalities of that language." At the same time, he was cautious surrounding himself with 500 of his men who were "armed with fuzees." He projected his confident and assertive personality and the English troops retreated (*R.* 32).

1763: According to the Treaty of Paris, Saint Vincent and Dominica Islands became English property. The English divided the Islands among themselves. This division produced an uprising of the unvanquished Black Caribs. Peace returned only when they succeeded to an agreement "that apparently satisfied the two disputing parties" (quoted by *R.* 33).

1773: The concluding definitive Treaty of Peace between representatives of the British Crown and the Caribs chiefs took place. The Caribs agreed to be taken to a reservation in the Islands, as well as, to the limitation of their territory; they also agreed to send back the fugitives, and to help the Crown against its enemies. On the other hand, according to the Crown laws, the English permitted them free trade such as fishing, etc. (cfr. *S.* 45 and *R.* 33).

1779: Helped by the French, the Black Caribs took the Island under control; they fought against the English forces who were engaged in the war that lead to the independence of the thirteen American colonies. The blacks' attack was what made the English surrender to the French without resistance (*S*. 45 and *R*. 33).

1783: Because of a treaty between France and England, the Island returned to the English who, in order to achieve peace, "overlooked the Caribs bad behavior. The Caribs were again confined to a reservation. But, they requested that the 1773 treaty must be honored" (*S*. 46 and *R*. 34). In this way, the Caribs Golden Age began in the beautiful island of "Lurumai"[3] or Saint Vincent. Prosperity manifested itself in investments for plantations, acquisition of slaves, wine, bread, European style home construction, and luxurious women's clothes (*R*. 34).

1795: Instigated by the French, and led by the head chief Chatoyé, the Black Caribs tried to take control of the Island. Chatoyé proclaimed allegiance to the French Revolution and to Victor Hughes, who was the especial delegate.

1796: In October, Spain and England declared war on each other (*R*. 36). The Black Caribs attacked the English plantations, but because of an old rivalry existing between the English black slaves and the Caribs, the black slaves formed an alliance with their masters in a fierce defense that permitted the English to gain precious time until the English troops arrived to impose a total victory. First, the General Marinier with his army capitulated in June. Later, despite devastating guerrilla warfare, and the help of people of color, the Black Caribs surrendered. There was a total of 5,000 Black Caribs and at least 1,000 supporters involved. Not all Black Caribs left Saint Vincent. Some of them sought refuge in the mountains. But, since they were such a small group that was not a threat in any way, little by little, they were accepted back by the English. In 1804 they were confined to Mone Ronda. In 1805 they received a total of 125 hectares of land,

---

3. Lurumai is the Garifuna name for Saint Vincent Island

which was evidence that the group was extremely reduced.[4] In 1812, the Volcano Suffriére eruption forced a big group of Caribs to emigrate to Trinidad. In 1887 when Ober visited the Island he found no more than 300 Black Caribs, dedicated to trading their products, transporting them in their canoes to the ships that arrived at the beaches.

There were several disastrous occurrences: a hurricane in 1898 and four years later, in 1902, another volcano eruption. Between 1950 and 1960 the Government favored the Caribs settlements in Petite Bordel and in New Sandy Bay. In 1971 and 1972 two volcano eruptions were expected and the Caribs were evacuated. However, the eruptions did not occur, and the Caribs returned. In 1974 they were in Paget Farm (Bequia Island), Greiggs, Rose Bank, Petit Bordel, Dark View, De Volet, Fancy, Owia Point, Old Sandy Bay and New Sandy Bay.[5]

1797: On March 11, 1797, the convoy "Experiment" with Captain Bannet in command prepared a convoy of ships with 5,080 defeated men and sent them to Roatan Island in Honduras Bay where they arrived on Wednesday, April 12, 1797 at 3:00 p.m.[6]

— Tegucigalpa 1798 quoting from (*"El Bitágora del Capitán del Convoy.*-Biblioteca Nacional de Inglaterra), (cfr. *S.* 46). The Spanish Crown was worried because of the English actions and requested that the Governor of Honduras, Coronel Anguiano, intervene in the matter. In May 1797, a considerable army at the command of Don José Rossi arrived in Roatan. They were welcomed by the Caribs with whom they made peace and who invited them to collaborate in the reconstruction of the city of Trujillo, once devastated by pirates. This is how another era began in the convoluted history of this town that has never submitted easily to foreign invaders.

---

4. Gullick in "The Carib at Saint Vincent a historical background and research bibliography" in *Belizean Studies*, Vol. 3, No. 3, May 1975, pp. 22-7. From now on as Gullick.

5. Gullick, with its respective map.

6. Armando Crisanto, *El pueblo Garifuna*, (polycopiado, p. 5).

CHAPTER 2

THE RELIGIOUS WORLD OF THE GARIFUNA[1]

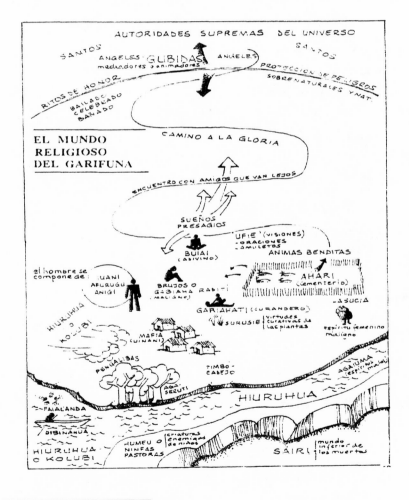

1. Taken from *RGAC*, pp. 101-26.

The religion of the Black Caribs is shaped by Roman-Catholic teachings and practices. They added inherited beliefs from African and native Indian ancestors to their rites with the objective of achieving the ascension of their dead relatives to a state of deification whereupon, they could be honored "as children should honor their parents." That is, to appease them if they are irritated with their living relatives and to ensure their good will and uninterrupted protection against natural and supernatural dangers. Therefore, in terms of practical implications, and to preserve group traditions, these beliefs should be regarded as the core of the Caribbean creed. Typical Carib virtues of flexibility and versatility allowed integration of this non-Christian tradition with Catholicism, acquiring with this integration, in spite of the vigorous protest of church representatives, a coherent union of values. In no other aspect have Garifuna culture, African, Indo American, and European elements been so totally integrated as in the elaboration of theological concepts, especially those which refer to the nature of the soul.

They have neither an ecclesiastical hierarchy, nor a well defined dogma, but rather beliefs that can be presented in the following way: Man's soul is composed of three parts:

ANIGI: Is a kind of vital force or animal spirit conceived as concrete identity but non substantial at the same time. It is centered in the heart and extinguishes itself either immediately after the death of its bearer or, at the most, after several months. A point of discussion is if the shadow, IAUA, is a direct projection from the body, UGUBU or ANIGI. Once past infancy, there is little or no concern at all for ANIGI. However, some illnesses that affect adults are also blamed on the ANIGI and are cured by a woman healer.

IUANI: Does not have a physical form. It is the second component of the soul, located in the head, and leaves the body immediately after death. It is not perceptible to the senses, and it is incapable of manifesting itself to the living (*RGAC*, 102-3). It would be equivalent to the Catholic concept of the "soul."

AFURUGU: Between the ANIGI and the spiritual IUANI it is the AFURUGU or literally "the other pair," which is an astral body that reproduces the physical material shape of the person in all details, but it is formed from a substance similar to the supernatural entities, sharing their personality traits. Along the life of a person, this entity does not have an independent existence. It is the intermediary between the kingdom of the supernatural and the kingdom of everyday reality. It advises its master of dangers through recognizable signal, such as itching on the arms, etc.

The beginnings of the stability that rules the Garifuna society is also basic for their religious life. That is why it is necessary to follow rules and religious practices so that the soul of the deceased can progress towards glory and reach higher positions in the world of the dead. This is a very slow and gradual process similar to reaching a position of security, pleasure, and well being on earth. After death, the soul goes to heaven or to purgatory. To help the soul to reach its final destiny only a few celebrations of mass are necessary.

The problem for the astral body or AFURUGU of the dead is that it stays on earth, due to the AHARI, the name given to those who just died. They are irritable and capricious. As a general rule they do not let their relatives see them but reveal their presence in the house through squeaking noises and slamming doors. They can cause domestic incidents. At night they wander around the town streets and can be seen by bystanders. These spirits are called ghosts or UFIE.

It is generally accepted that a year and a half after death, the astral body of the dead (AFURUGU) begins its journey with its soul (IUANI) to a permanent resting place, after bathing (AMUIEDAHANI) several times and having celebrated (ACUGUHANI) and danced (ADOGORAHANI) with earthly relatives.

The journey toward the world of the after life is long and difficult and on their way the spirits of the dead ask for more baths to refresh themselves, and food offerings to gain strength. Eventually, if they are not retained in an "evil" place, even the slowest AHARI will arrive to its final destiny. The surviving relatives are informed of the progress of the trip through dreams and premonitions, until the spirit is united with GUBIDA.

In the Caribs hierarchy, the GUBIDA are on the same level as the Angels. The term "lonely soul" is applied to those who are in purgatory and occupy one place after saints, various virgins and ancestors. Therefore, they can have access to these when they intercede in favor of their living relatives.

GUBIDA favor their relatives but, also, if these do not comply with the religious rites in their honor, Gubida can harm them. Gubida can also harm the relatives if they violate group traditions.

At first, interactions between a fortune teller (BUIA)) and the spirits of the ancestors are never done directly but through other spirits called HIURUHA, who occupy an inferior position in relation to ancestors. It is believed that some of the HIURUHA live in the lower region of the kingdom of the dead, called SAIRI, which refers to the island that the Caribs consider as paradise, although sometimes it is identified with limbo of Catholic theology.

The majority of the BUIAI call upon HIURUHA or KOLUBI, the spiritual entities that assist them in their "work." These spiritual assistants act as messengers between the fortune tellers (BUIAI) and the ancestors; they reveal the reasons why they are irritated by their living relatives; they ask ancestors to come down to discuss the matter with their relatives and invite them to be in the religious ceremonies celebrated in their honor.

HIURUHA also help religious practitioners find the causes of an illness and help them to prescribe the appropriate medicine; they discover "intrigues" that their enemies have arranged with the help of a witch, or reveal hidden supernatural impediments to a marriage; they also give magic powers to fetishes; all in all, they guarantee the success of the BUIAI in favor of their client.

There are many spirits watching the life of the Garifunas. In rivers, several water falls are refuge to AGAIUMA, fantastic beings that can appear in a shape of a crocodile or a crab, but in general they take the appearance of a beautiful woman with fair skin and green hair, (*RGAC*, p. 110).

SUCIA: Is a feminine spirit that could be harmful to the young. It originates in a cemetery, apparently coming from the vital energy (ANIGI) of a woman who died under strange conditions. Others say that she comes from any accumulated decomposed organic material. She leaves at midnight and presents herself to men under the image of an attractive woman, who lure them far away until she turns herself into an ugly old witch.

One can find the DIBIMAHUA in the sea through the fishermen. DIBIMAHUA is a being that turns canoes upside down when it is angry. It is known as the HIURUHUA of the sea or the FAIALANDA.

The FAIALANDA is very often described as a light that can be seen at a great distance. Some fishermen claim having seen the contours of an ancient ship illuminated by such light. Taylor is probably right when he finds the origins of this belief in the European legend of the "El holandés errante"[2] which was introduced to the West Indies by the seamen of the seventeenth century.

It is believed that the sea is also the dwelling place of the UMEU, small creatures who hate children, (*RGAC*, p. 111). They are also called "pastoral nymphs."

OGOREU: Is a supernatural evil who attaches to women and is transmitted through the maternal line. OGOREU is generally seen, in the shape of a blue alligator, but he can also appear as a crab, snake, armadillo or any other small animal. He is also known as ULASA, a word of Miskito origin which, according to one theory, refers to a particular kind of OGOREU.

MAFIA: They are spirits who wonder the streets at night; sometimes, they enter the houses and are responsible for domestic accidents. Their leader is UINANI, often identified with Satan.

Lone travelers refer to these encounters as grotesque animals appearing at the outskirts of villages. It seems that these creatures become enlarged when someone approaches them, and seconds later they vanish in thin air. For example, TIMBO, a canine-spirit and CADEJO, a feline-spirit, belong to this category. The

---

2. The "Holandés Errante" is a seaman from Holland whose ship could not continue the trip because of a lack of wind in one of his trips to the Indies. He was trapped for so long that he decided to make a pact with the devil. He surrendered his soul to the devil in exchange for wind. Since then the "Holandés Errante" wanders the seas pushed by the wind of the devil. *www.sable.esmartweb.com/relatos.html*

HURUHA or LOLUBI are personifications of the natural forces known as AGAIUMA and DIBINAHUA. The latter, together with the animal spirits such as the CADEJO and the TIMBO, can be designated with the collective expression: LABUREME UBAO.[3] Another phrase, LIHORO UBAO,[4] includes the ones just mentioned and SUCIA, FAIALANDA, UMEU, OGOREU, IA ARARU GU and MAFIA. Some Caribs maintain that these two phrases, "Labureme Ubao" and "Lihoro Ubao" are interchangeable.

DUNDES and PENGALIBA are two other kinds of spirits identified with the demons of Catholicism. They live in big trees and are sought by ambitious people or by those who are in a desperate economic situation and are willing to sign a pact with the spirits.

The Catholic traditions brought by the Spanish colonizers to Honduras needed little change to be assimilated by the religious minds of Black Caribs. It was supposed that saints owed respect to their devotees and that candles lit for them and prayers said in their names are a kind of payment in advance for requested favors.

There are saints who are "specialists" in providing protection against specific type of maladies or problems and, in this sense, Caribs practices are identical to Iberian[5] traditions. Among Caribs one can find associations, sororities, fraternities and religious organizations representing the most visible aspects of the religious life of all Central American population.

Elderly women are the ones who most actively participate in the cult of the dead. They are also members of religious associations, but they must keep in secret their participation in ceremonies that are prohibited by the Church. If an ecclesiastic authority finds out about such activity this could be a reason for an immediate expulsion from the organization. However, there is little or no fear of denunciation because almost all members of the association are guilty of the same transgression.

---

3. Abureme: landlord. Ubao: island, land, village.
4. Afflictions or nightmares of the earth or towns.
5. Iberian: pertaining to Spain.

As a general rule Black Caribs do not neglect devotion to saints, even though, according to their concept Catholicism, the saints are distant and less directly interested in human affairs than ancestors and evil spirits. However, Caribs try to associate every important event in their life with both, spirits and saints, GUBIDA, because, according to a proverb, "one never has enough rum, enough money, or enough protectors from the above.

Each family transmits to relatives magic formulas called prayers and those who practice professional magic and have the capability of transforming their physical appearance into an animal or plant are denominated BURUHU (from the Spanish 'brujo').[6]

Prayers are good for several purposes: to take revenge upon an enemy, to find out about the future, to find lost objects, or to regain health. There is no distinction between prayers addressed to evil spirits from those invoking protection from Saint Anthony, Saint Cyprian, and other Saints.

In general, it is accepted that certain objects can be "loaded with witchcraft" (ABIARAGOLE) and are capable of producing destructive effects without the help of a spiritual agent. Objects used for protection against witchcraft are called IARI (COLLARS). This term can be applied to religious medals, saints relics or scapulars containing written prayers, which are distributed by Catholic priests. However, more often, they refer to amulets or lucky charms, (LUIAUANURA) made by the BUIAI. Other fetishes protect houses, boats, and plantations. In addition to serving as protection against black magic, the IARI have another positive role; for example, they contribute to the success of all enterprises.

Magic is important in the life of the Caribs, and it is also attractive to those who are not directly interested in religious issues. Love filters and spells are used for specific purposes and their preparation (UAIARU) is the most profitable activity of magic professionals.

---

6. Brujo: Wizard.

CHAPTER 3

BLACKS IN BELIZE

Belize, a small piece of land of 23,043 square kilometers,[1] with less than 150,000 inhabitants, was chosen for invasion by Guatemala and El Salvador. The invasion was supposed to take place on Friday, February 4, 1972. "The English counted the chickens before they hatched," because one year before, in 1971, England had announced the independence of Belize. Due to an old misinterpreted treaty between Guatemala and England in 1859, Guatemala was to keep Belizean territory which was considered to be "one of its provinces." On the other hand, during the following ten years, 500,000 Salvadorans went to Belize, but England and English and American enterprises, which controlled 90% of Belize's land, knew that it was possible to import grass and exploit the wood industry. They also knew that there were petroleum wells in the south of the Toledo Province. Moreover, from Belize they could control business throughout the Caribbean. All this was more than enough reason for England to send 3,000 seamen, a fleet of eighteen Harrier planes, and the plane carrier Ark Royal to anchor in the sea of Belize.

The invasion did not take place and Belize became independent, due most of all to the work of George Price who had struggled against English colonialism from 1950 to 1964 until the decision to fight for independence was made.

From 1964 on, he fought against the ongoing efforts of Guatemala to gain control over this land.[2] In September 21, 1981 at 12 noon, the tricolor, blue, white and red, flag was raised and Belize became the last Central American

---

1.   2.590 Km^2 = 1sq. mile
2.   The "Order of National Hero" medal was awarded to George Price on Tuesday, September 19, 2000. He was honored as the father of [the] Nation in recognition of his value to Belize as a citizen and as a leader. *http://bleaseswebworld.com/gprice.html*

country to gain independence. Belize's journey to find a place among other nations of the world began; up until that moment, it had been unknown as a country. In fact, it had been called "British Honduras."

It is interesting to observe what the Guatemalan army had planned to do with Belize and its people. According to the declarations of Colonel Rene Mendoza, presidential aid to General Kjell Lauregud García, the intentions were as follows: "We are neither unreasonable nor opinionated. The development of Peten (frontier region) depends on the control of Belize; regarding the problem of the elimination of the foreign populations the solution will be that at least blacks should be deported. They are not Guatemalan citizens but descendants of those who invaded the country. As simple as that, we will send them back to the land of their ancestors."[3]

As a good army man, Colonel Rene Mendoza was explicit. Although articulate, he lacked historical accuracy. He had been chosen by Guatemala and El Salvador for the invasion of Belize.

Who were the blacks who would be sent back to their land? First of all, they were 60% of Belize population; the rest were Maya Indians, mestizos, Asians, and 3% were Europeans, a variety of races living in peace, thanks to a wise policy of governance. Let's consider the two black groups in Belize:

1.) The GARIFUNA or GARINAGUA, called also black Caribs, are 15% of the black population of the country, but they have special characteristics. Lately they have been very active and present in national life from politics to religion. Let's not forget that at the time the only Catholic Bishop living in Belize City was Monsignor Franklin Martin, who was black and was the only titular black Bishop of all Central and South America.

Until 1800, the history of black Caribs was the same as the Garifunas which spread from Belize through all of Guatemala, Honduras and Nicaragua. They have been in Belize since 1802. A. Cunningham, an English

---

3.   Published in the *Expansión de México Magazine*, October 2, 1974.

Representative, annoyed by the presence of 150 Garifunas, requested their expulsion from the country.

Many blacks were involved in smuggling and worked in the exportation of fine wood. Their relationship with the British Governor was somehow always tense. They were threatened and expelled, but returned later and things continued as before. In 1807 a group of these blacks was sent to Cayo Coker Fort; in 1811 the superintendent of the Fort threatened the Caribs with expulsion if they did not present permits of residence within forty-eight hours. Thus the settlement of Stann Creek began in 1820, where traditions rooted. Threats of expulsion continued with many alternatives and only in 1857 did they receive permits to stay permanently in Stann Creek or in Dangriga.

Jesuits have been the preachers of Belize. They also arrived in Livingston, Guatemala, and in other small Garifuna cities. They owned St. John College, the main college of Belize City. Jesuits were influential in educational and cultural investigations. (There were no universities in the country at that time). Father Richard Buller S.J. studied in depth the language of the Garifunas, and published an enriching and comprehensive dictionary. But, in reality, with the exception of the work of Dr. Joseph Palacios, an anthropologist, who earned his Ph.D. degree with a thesis on "The Religion and Language of the Garifuna," this group had not been sufficiently studied and investigated; that is why they are barely known.

Professor Jerry Valentino, a Garifuna proud of his culture and traditions, was also proud of being Catholic like the majority of his people. Sometimes he experienced tension between the two religions, mainly because the Church accused him of being too linked with the Garifuna religion or superstitions. On the other hand, the Garifuna elders said that he was siding with the Catholic priests. In other words, he was a "bridge" between two religions. He spoke with conviction about the values and the liturgy of the Garifunas who had already adopted the Catholic mass. He said that on "The Day of the Garifuna," Bishop Martin was going to celebrate the mass in his language.

His parents used to live in Belize. They were a nice elderly couple, still active and strong, yet unaware of the grace God had given them, a son who was not only a priest but a Bishop.

According to Professor Valentino, the Garifuna people still follow their "priests" with interest in ceremonies celebrated to free the souls. These ceremonies make it possible for the soul to reach heaven, so that they can assist the Garifuna people to cure diseases and interpret events.

The Garifuna have strong organizational skills. This is shown not only by the existence of numerous Garifuna sports teams but also by group organizations such as the Young Men Sporting Association "Star Ling" which invited us to participate in interesting Antillean dances with Jamaican and Haitian influences. One of these performances took place during the celebration of the Association's thirty-sixth anniversary.

There are also cultural groups and social advancement groups, such as the "Caribbean Development Society," although the government does not always like these groups.

Actually, the most enduring Garifuna Association is the "National Garifuna Council." Its secretary is Sebastian Gayetano who directs, through Radio Belize, a radio program in Garifuna language every Sunday.

According to Professor Joseph Palacio, an interesting fact is that almost twice of the Garifuna population of Belize have emigrated to various cities of the United States, such as New York, Chicago, and Los Angeles where they also have their associations.

In the last few years, a desire to build a relationship with Garifuna communities of other countries of Central America has flourished, and new encouragement toward the study and appreciation of their culture has sprouted. This will be an indispensable factor for the Garifuna to rediscover and assert their identity. It will empower them to participate as protagonists in the historic process of their countries and of their ethnic group, enriching in this way their specific cultural contributions to Latin America and the world.

2.) CREOLES are the largest group of blacks in Belize. They comprise 40% of the population and live mainly in Belize City, the ancient capital, and not in Belmopan, the new Belizean capital, built inland as protection against always imminent storms and tornadoes. Creoles speak English, the official national language that is taught in all schools, but in general they speak a kind of dialect, mixed with English, Castilian and other words taken from different ethnic groups.

In addition to English, the majority of the people speak at least one other language fluently such as Castilian, Mayan, Chinese, or German; Garifuna literacy is high, reaching 90%. More than half of the population professes Catholicism, the rest are protestant of different denominations.

In general people are poor, but the welfare organization "Partido Unido del Pueblo" has secured food, basic health services, and shelter. For many, in places such as Belize city, these needs continue to be a problem for a number of people.

Where do the Creoles come from? First, let's say that from the third to the tenth century of our era, the Mayans dominated in Belize territory, then mysteriously disappeared. During the sixteenth and seventeenth centuries, Spaniards were not interested in this region; they paid sporadic visits. Even missionaries were not interested in this territory.

On the other hand, this zone, with its numerous series of Coral Islands named "Cayo" and several small rivers, especially the estuary at the end of the Belize River, attracted the attention of pirates who sought refuge here after their plunder. They lived in peace with their people and other adventurers, among them black fugitive and free slaves. These buccaneers, who Emilio Salgari used to call "The Coast Brothers," settled there permanently little by little, turning themselves into hard working colonizers. They brought slaves from Jamaica and the Antilles because manual labor was needed to work in the woods, cutting trees, and removing them, especially the ebony trees. Manual labor was also needed to help build prosperous farms.

In reality, it was difficult to say who was in charge. During the seventeenth and eighteenth centuries, in some sense, these people considered

44

England their mother country, but Spain interference caused diplomatic problems. Every so often, the Spaniards started an armed fight. At the turn of the nineteenth century this frontier site turned officially into the colony of "British Honduras.

The fate of the slaves was hard. They lived in sub- human conditions and therefore rebelled on several occasions. At the same time their attempted uprisings were oppressed in bloody ways. Some succeeded in escaping to regions dominated by the Spaniards where laws were lenient although there was also some oppression. But, in spite of the hazardous living conditions, the black population was always larger than the European population.

With time, Spaniards initiated internal laws in the Popular Assembly. They democratically elected authorities such as magistrates who had executive and judicial functions for a period of one year. The Spaniards' attempts to deport the English and the African people failed and the Spaniards were repelled in the Battle of St. George, on September 10, 1798.

They did not attempt a military coup again but initiated a series of diplomatic intrigues through treaties that were never enforced.

During the eighteenth century only whites could be in the Popular Assembly. Participation of free blacks was permitted in 1808. A sovereign decree "permitting all common citizens, colored people of free status, to have the same rights and privileges of the British born, or of those born from white parents" was approved in 1831. A law of 1838 confirmed that "it was true that men of color could occupy the magistrate seat but could not act like a magistrate or juror." The fact is that with the arrival of the English representative in 1784, the Assembly became weak.

In 1826, English authorities including General Good often blamed Guatemala for the fact that a lot of blacks escaped to their territory. With the abolition of slavery in 1834, blacks could vote providing they fulfilled certain requirements. Due to the fact that blacks were overwhelmingly superior in number to Europeans, they were considered a threat if the plebiscite continued. For this reason, the Popular Assembly was dissolved in 1854 and a constitution creating a four year Legislative Assembly was established. Members of this assembly needed to own property valued at 400 pounds or more. England always supported the interests of the whites. For example in 1809 the English government rejected the proposal to form a Council with elected members. It was clear that of the 30,000 inhabitants at that time, only 400 were of European descent.

In the twentieth century, Belize continued under English protectorate and in 1929 an economic crisis (in addition to the 1931 hurricane) obliged the country to seek help from England. England accepted, but on condition that the British Governor would be the sole authority. He assumed power in 1932. During this time a group of Afro-Belizeans who wanted to participate more actively in political decisions emerged. Because at that time all power was in the hands of the Governor, their wish to participate in politics was granted.

From the 1950s up until the 1980s, Belizeans started a movement towards power, with the activities of the two groups, the UPM[4] and the PUP,[5] until they gained independence. Unfortunately, Manuel Esquivel, the new minister of the PUP, was getting dangerously close to the politics of Ronald Reagan and favored a USA military and economic intervention which would have had detrimental consequences to the peace of this small and hard working country, an island of tranquility in the stormy Central American sea.

---

4. UPM: United People's Movement.
5. PUP: People United Party. Today as UDP: United Democratic Party.

SETTLEMENTS OF BLACK CARIBS IN CENTRAL AMERICA

1. Stann Creek	19. Cayo Venado	37. Santa Rosa de Aguán
2. Hopkins	20. Rosita	38. Limó
3. Georgetown	21. Monte Pobre	39. Punta de Piedra
4. Seine Bight	22. Punta Gorda	40. Cusuna
5. Punta Gorda	23. Corozal	41. Ciriboya
6. Barranco	24. Sambo Creek	42. Iriona Viejo
7. Quebesh	25. Nueva Armenia	43. San José de la Punta
8. Livingston	26. Salado Lis-Lis	44. Iriona
9. Masca	27. Balfate	45. Sangrelaya
10. Travesia	28. Rio Esteban	46. Cocalito
11. Bajamar	29. Guadalupe	47. Tocomacho
12. Saragüina	30 San Antonio	48. San Pedro
13. Rio Tinto	31. Santa Fe	49. Batalla
14. Tornabé	32. Cristales	50. Pueblo Nuevo
15. San Juan	33. Rio Negro	51. Plapaya
16. La Ensenada	34. Barranco Blanco	52. Orinoco
17. Triunfo de la Cruz	35. Barra de Chapagua	53. La Fe
18. Nuevo Go	36. Barra de Aguán	

CHAPTER 4

BLACKS IN GUATEMALA

Situation of the Afro-Guatemalan Population
(Livingston and Puerto Barrios-IZABAL)

The black population in Guatemala is located mainly in Livingston and Puerto Barrios, in the department of IZABAL, on the Atlantic Coast. According to statistics, there are 142,000 people of color in the whole country. Blacks of Guatemala distinguish among themselves according to the history of each group:

— Blacks of the colonial era who worked in the mines.

— "Culies," the result of the mixture between blacks and Indians (from India); they arrived during the times of British influence, mainly during the Second World War. An elderly man used to say that the "Culies" were "blacks with straight hair like the natives of the country."

The black population in Guatemala is divided mainly in these two groups: Blacks from colonial times and Culies. The *Christian Encyclopedia* registers a population of approximately 142,000 of these two groups in 1980.

In addition to these two groups, there exists another one, and because it is a majority it deserves a special attention: the Garifuna group.

Livingston is a big town at the mouth of the Dulce River, on the Atlantic Coast with a population of no more than 2,000 people. Until today, the population of Livingston was mainly Garifuna. They arrived in Guatemala at the turn of the nineteenth century.

Elder Antonio Sánchez, one of the recognized keepers of the old Garifuna traditions, proudly states that the first person to arrive in Livingston, then called

Boca Grande or "Buga," was his ancestor Marcos Sánchez Díaz, who had left Honduras and arrived in Livingston on November 9, 1802.

Continuing their traditions until today, the Garifunas earn their living primarily from fishing, hunting and to a lesser extent from agriculture. All those who spoke to us maintained that one of the more serious problems on the island is the lack of jobs. As a result, people emigrate in particular to the USA: New York, Los Angeles and other cities such as in Texas[1] where they do domestic work. The most fortunate join the Navy, work in factories or go to school. Very often, they have documentation problems, and for that reason they try to enter the country clandestinely, usually through Mexico. Many of them, especially those with "resident" status, send money from the USA to help their families.

The typical Garifuna meals are: "Tapado con harina dorada" which is a fried fish with coconut and tobago,[2] curete,[3] macue,[4] shrimp and jaiba;[5] the "tamale," prepared with green plantain, coconut milk, beef broth, yuca[6] and banana that the Garifunas cultivate themselves. The "barbecue" is also among the typical dishes. The basic staple food is "rice and beans." The Garifuna dances are: "Punta Crepes," "Yancunu," etc. Catholicism had been, and still is, the center of the religious and social life of the Garifunas.

The first priests were Jesuits who established themselves permanently in Livingston, in 1865. They came from Belize, and the rectory in Livingston was built around 1906.

There exist a series of strong traditions related to religious festivities such us: Holy Week, Saint Isidoro (in May), the Virgin (in October), Saint Raphael, and Saint Michael.

These festivities were very important occasions for expressing religious beliefs, popular faith, and social life. Proof of these are the Fraternity Associations that influenced their civil life. For example, the Jesus Nazareno

---

1. Texas City, in South East Texas, on Galveston Bay.
2. Tobago: sea food
3. Curete: a fish
4. Macue: sea food
5. Jaiba: crustacean , a kind of crab.
6. Edible tuberous root similar to cassava

Fraternity was in charge of all church festivities. Its members prepared and organized the events and worked in common agreement with the priest.

During Holy Week members of this Fraternity had the privilege of carrying a statue of Christ in a procession. They had to wear the proper attire: black pants, and black jacket, white shirt and a very big white handkerchief, which was used to touch Christ.

According to Mister Cristóbal, the butler, Saint Raphael Fraternity had ten to fifteen members who gathered together with the director every week to organize the Saint Raphael festivity. During the weekly reunions they used to examine monthly projects, and sometimes organized "milpas," a communal rice planting that was harvested and cooked for the festivity. In this way they consolidated their relationship and at the same time created a spirit of solidarity.

The Garifunas keep their traditions today, especially those related with the cult to the dead. Those who are not familiar with the Garifuna religion look at these practices with distrust and hate. One "Ladino"[7] or white from town said: "They practice too many exotic customs from Africa. Their language is a mixture of French and their native African language; they play drums too much and believe in Voodoo and witchcraft . . ." They keep these in their unconscious because the majority have become Christians, and in Voodoo they believe in the spirits, mixing ancestral beliefs with Christian elements.

Concerning political power, the Garifunas maintain that several years ago when positions were still honorary and there was nothing to gain from them, they were in charge. Then things changed. Now, the "Ladinos" are in charge. They turn to blacks only to obtain their vote during elections. Some stated that on several occasions they were manipulated, especially when there were black puppet candidates, like Mariano Blanco. But, in general, the Garifunas are not conscious of the need to participate in politics, and are not yet organized. Things are different in the United States where black's voice is to a certain extent being heard.

---

7. See Introduction, footnote number 3.

In spite of the odds, Mr. Roberto Mejía became secretary of publicity during the time of Arévalo; Belisario Martínez was deputy, and Patricio Lorenzo became Mayor of Livingston; he had great popular support. Other famous men among Garifunas of Livingston and Puerto Barrios were in the army. Luciano Arzá was a captain who used to speak Garifuna dialect, as well as English, Castilian and some French. There were professors such as Pedro Espinoza, P. Ortiz, and Pacífico Lorenzo who served in the government, and Bonifacio Romero who organized Puerto Barrios. In sports there were David Stok, a football player; Mario Gamboa, a boxer, and Stella Zuñiga, a marathon runner.

The Garifuna group tried to respond to the realities of their social conditions through different kinds of popular organizations, such as "Amistad," "América" and "Grupo Unión" all organized by Franciscan priest P. Alonso Alayo from Livingston. The "Martínez Society" was organized by a Honduran of Masonic inspiration. (He had gone to Belize, where he formed part of a Masonic Association, and went back to live in Guatemala; he also organized the Martínez Association in Livingston). Then, the "Sociedad Juvenil" of Luis Franzúa emerged, which was eventually dissolved; Vicente Bonilla founded the "Alegría Society," and Patricio Lorenze began the "Social Club of Paris." There were also several sports and dance clubs such as the "Yancunu" dance group directed by Fernando Rojas and the "Uguger" of Doña Patrocinia Sánchez. All these groups were characterized by their instability and short duration. There were also cooperatives, formed mainly by fishermen, which were made up of black members because 90% of them were dedicated to fishing and they knew their trade very well.

The best known organization was, without any doubt, the ASO-Garifuna Association founded January 6, 1981 by Bonifacio Núñez who became its coordinator. It started with twenty members. The primary objective of this organization was to improve the situation of blacks in Guatemala. At that time, the members of this Association were 50% blacks, the rest were whites and mestizos. Some people said: "Garifuna means black. Therefore, to say ASO-Garifuna is the same as saying 'Dark Peoples Movement'." Others say: "The term Garifuna makes them understand the origin of their race. It has to do more with race consciousness and not with being black or mulatto." This Association was directed at that time by Sir Luis Franzúa, a dark man in his fifties, strong and stocky, with a wide smile and keen eyes. He said about himself:

> I was a seaman for ten years. I know Santo Domingo, the Caribbean, and I am happy to have been acquainted with so many places and be able to tell my people what is going on in those locations. The fact of being in contact with colored people, black like me, and talk to them to overcome the problems concerning our race, makes me feel proud.

His speech continued:

> The ASO-Garifuna Association was founded in order to respond to people's necessities in work, agriculture, and fishing. For a very long time we heard that blacks were in charge of several public positions until they turned into honorary activities. When these activities became paid positions, blacks were ignored. We are claiming our rights as Guatemalans, and we want to let the government know that we also exist here.
> Through the ASO-Garifuna Association we were able to obtain a sea dock in Livingston, an ambulance, and a budget for a tourist center. We also presented to the Minister of Government all work problems that young students were facing; then we asked for judicial personnel who can defend us in a court of law.
> The Association had 130 members with at least 45 permanent participants. We went ahead with a program sponsored by the 'World Children' a USA organization for the welfare of poor children. A black woman said: 'We help affiliated poor children. We take a picture of them and send it to the main house in New York. Over there the people in charge find godparents who will send money for food, medicine and clothing and we deliver a 'family basket' containing some basic nutritious food: maize, milk, flour, and rice. Every six months we pay them a doctor's visit. Soon we will have a dentist.'

Don Luis Franzúa said that this project had been going on for a year. They wanted to add classes for parents and, if possible, get a loan for each child. There were 800 hundred children registered in the program!

He continued:

More than that, we want to direct our attention to a problem that usually people want to hide, and it is occurring even among blacks themselves in black neighborhoods, which is a sad truth today in Guatemala. We are talking about racial discrimination present in the whole country. From 1950 to 1968, there were only colored people in Puerto Barrios docks. Then they were laid off with the excuse that the company went bankrupt. In reality it had to do with the racial problem! We are repudiated here because of the color of our skin, but what they can not tolerate is that we come from the same race of the Arawak Indians.

A few months ago we presented a project for a loan to INACOP and after waiting for a long time, we were told in a meeting that people from Livingston should forget about the loan. I asked them why? They responded that when blacks from Livingston have money they spend it and do nothing productive with it. I answered that if we do not get either technical assistance or insights on how to make a profit with the money, things become complicated not only for blacks but also for whites.

We were able to participate in the 'Coordinadora,' in the assembly of the main authorities of the region; among the members of the assembly were the Governor of the Department, the Commander in Chief of the Navy, the Lieutenant of the Base, and one representative for each of the following: IFA,[8] Fire Brigade, and the Red Cross.

On the other hand, some "Ladinos" say:

The Garifunas are economically poor, and they do not worry about advancement or about the future of their children. Sometimes they have three women; if they get three or four fish, one is for each woman, and the last one is sold to buy alcoholic beverages. They do not persevere, nor worry to save money, but only save for annual parties. They work to get money for new outfits. This is just pure fun.

The Aso-Garifuna Association would like to push the black group toward cooperation with other black populations from Belize, Honduras and elsewhere in Latin America. The president of the Institution used to say: "Soon we will have an assembly about this topic in Honduras, which will be organized by OFRANEH

---

8.   Instituto de Formación Afroecuatoriana.

(Organización Fraternal Negra Hondureña)[9] although the problem of discrimination will not be eliminated."

Elsy Zuñiga, a national student athlete, explains these problems in the following way:

> I believe that here in our country discrimination is much more serious than in North America. Over here there are no jobs in enterprises for colored people. We take exams and we are not even informed immediately about negative decisions. Instead we are harassed until we stop pursuing the matter. Meanwhile, they have already hired the candidates. Then, they take the chosen employees to the capital.
> There are no more than five natives working in business enterprises of the area. We are always mistreated with negative attitudes or with verbal offenses. In elementary schools black children are ignored. However, discrimination in high schools is less severe and some blacks are able to go to college and become professionals such as architects, medical doctors and lawyers. On the other hand, there are no jobs in banks for blacks. In the Bank of Guatemala there is only one black, working as a guard. There are only menial jobs for blacks in the army. There was only one black Cleretiano priest, Milton Álvarez, who was in Africa at the time.

Blacks in Guatemala are less important than the rest of the population. They are considered a folkloric or traditional element, useful for advertisements to attract tourists to Livingston and Puerto Barrios. They have lost ground in economic, political and administrative issues. Different associations, including the ASO-GARIFUNA association revealed, among other things, a desire for solidarity and unification before a world and old traditions that are disappearing due to lack of privacy. The Garifunas have lost the isolation that previously protected them. Because of business enterprises interested in making profit, the Garifunas have been forced out of their traditional villages. Now blacks have to courageously confront an uncertain and difficult future by fighting competitive employees who make alliances with mestizo colonizers.

Obstacles worth noting are: lack of strong leaders who can provide union and consciousness to the group, ignorance of cultural origins which contributes to

---

9. Honduran Black Fraternal Organization.

the weak identity of the group, and differences in ways of understanding economic growth (more in function of the individual than collectively). These impediments contribute to slow the advancement of a group of people that has very important cultural values to contribute to the society of Guatemala.

If we observe the way other ethnic minorities have been treated in Guatemala, especially the indigenous groups -some have already disappeared, others are at the verge of extinction, — we will have a "taste of death" that African groups may have the possibility of overcoming because of their vitality and strong desire for life and freedom.

CHAPTER 5

BLACKS IN HONDURAS

The Garifuna Population

Trujillo

Trujillo is a small and attractive city located on the green hills of the Honduran gulf on the Atlantic Coast. It is considered the center of the Garifuna population of Honduras.

In fact, this is the place where the Garifunas first arrived at the end of the eighteenth century. Those who came from Roatan Island with the approval of Spanish authorities settled in Central America where they have continued with their traditional hunting, fishing and agriculture. Little by little, they spread along the coast, reaching the North of Guatemala (Livingston, Puerto Barrios) and Belize (Dangriga). Trujillo continues to be the moral center of this ethnic group. This also includes the following towns: Ceiba, Tela, Puerto Cortes and Masca. Down to the south the Garifuna population predominates on the Coast until Iriona in Plaplaya. In Nicaragua they reach Puerto Cabezas, Laguna de Las Perlas, and the Zone of Bluefields.

In Honduras, the Garifuna population is perhaps at least 90,000 people, and they are aware of the necessity to advance. They believe that they need to struggle along a long road toward self identity and stability in order to find a proper place in the Honduran society.

In spite of differences among groups of Garifuna in small villages as well as bigger towns, including the capital itself, a sense of dignity, the will to actively participate in the history of the nation, and the nobility of the Garifuna are immediately noticed by any visitor.

Garifuna traditions are alive in the small city of Trujillo, which is the main center of this ethnic group in Honduras, and a point of reference for all Garifunas from Belize to Honduras. This is because Trujillo is one of the main ports of the country on the Atlantic Coast.

The majority of the population in Trujillo is black of Garifuna origin. But, the Ladino population has increased enormously in the past few years, and they control most business enterprises. Because they are supported by the central authorities, they can easily contest economic, administrative and political powers. A certain harmony can be observed, among inter-ethnic relationships, but it is difficult to say to what degree this harmony is authentic. Because the Ladinos are a minority, it is disadvantageous for them to show any feelings of racial superiority they may harbor against Garifunas.

There are two traditional black neighborhoods in Trujillo: "Cristales" and "Rio Negro," both on the ocean, surrounded by green thick vegetation where one can find beautiful, small, cozy houses, painted in good taste, and covered by green vegetation and coconut trees.

Streets are made of rough hard soil or irregular rocks. Schools are located on a Garifuna land, property obtained as a reimbursement for the territory that the government took away to build Puerto Castilla. A fort constructed by the Spaniards to defend themselves from frequent and disastrous pirate invasions is located on the high part of the city, the most strategic dominating position. Here is the grave of William Walker, a famous pirate who was executed on September 12, 1860.

During the Spanish era and for a long time thereafter, Trujillo city was the capital of Central America. But, because of frequent pirate assaults that occurred when cargos of gold and spices were ready to be sent to Spain, the location of the higher colonial authority was transferred. Building capital cities far from the sea to avoid pirate attacks became common practice in Latin America.

Cristales and Rio Negro are the oldest and most powerful communities as almost all political and administrative positions in local organizations are given to Ladinos. Members of these local organizations must pay dues, collaborate and participate in all big events of the community. They are in charge of organizing traditional dance performances during Christmas, Holy Week and Patron Saint festivities. Dancers wear traditional outfits and ornaments reminiscent of the Bahia candomble and the macumba of Rio de Janeiro in Brazil. They also play traditional musical instruments in these celebrations.

Township of Limon

At the entrance of the township of Limon in the rural area (Department of Colon) one can see small, beautiful and cozy one story houses built with guadua cane[1] with zinc roofs, although there are also some houses built of cement. They are spread throughout the rich green vegetation, with the sea in the background and the waves landing on a nearby beach. The Garifunas cannot be happy if they are not near the sea. They conduct their lives with dignity, and one can observe that everyone is busy doing some work.

The church is a big brick building, symbol of the Garifunas devotion to the Catholic faith they embraced when they arrived in Central America at the turn of the nineteenth century. Their main religious festivity is the Feast of the Immaculate Conception.

The school is another fundamental pillar for this community. Its members are proud of their traditions and of the outstanding people such as General Lorenzo Lacayo who became a successful professional. He was a carpenter at first, but attained prosperity. He participated in several insurrections. On three occasions, as the leader, he conquered the Military Plaza of Trujillo, "not for his benefit but as a protest against the injustices of that time and to put in positions of power people who he believed will do good deeds for the group." Another person worth mentioning was Pedro Medrano, one of the elders of the town. He was a good natured black man of medium height with white hair. He worked for the United Fruit Company and kept in his mind the "collective memory" of the "Garifuna arrival: people who came from St. Vincent and settled in Limon."

---

1. Guadua cane: A kind of bamboo used to build houses.

Groups

A Ladino female professor described the Garifunas as follows: "When blacks have their meetings and organize celebrations meditating on their ancestors, they sing in Garifuna, dance and do other things they cannot do anymore in downtown churches." The same female professor stressed the Garifuna's ability to organize groups with strong ties. She also said that, even those who emigrate, for example to the United States, continue their contributions to the economy of the town. She added: "Sometimes they seem quiet, but in their organizations and meetings they participate actively. I think that there are some problems when meetings are organized only for them. This is because they want to succeed and improve but do not want to share their progress with Ladinos. However, we have to recognize that they are very good, sincere and friendly people."

The "Frente Social Limoneño" is an organization formed by members from Limon who live in other countries, especially in the USA. They help not only their town but also others who need assistance, even if they do not belong to the community. For example, when there was a collection of money and lottery for the construction of the church; they also expected contributions from the members of the "Frente Social Limoneño."

Other typical sponsor organizations are dance groups or reunions such as the "Yunorini" for Lent. Others are of a socio-economic type such as the "Sociedad Los Hermanos," which was in its prime during the 1940s and owned a department store and a sailing ship.

In other Garifuna towns the elderly complain because young people "do not follow traditions and speak in Ladino not Garifuna." In Limon traditions are maintained by special religious rites, through dances, such as the "cupita," "maipol," "mascaros." Tradition is also practiced by groups such as the "Crisis Group" later named "Gafaifa," and "Los Quinientos."

Garifunas and Politics

Currently the progressive wing is the one directly involved in politics. Some are connected with political parties in search of immediate advantages during electoral campaigns. There are also others who nominate black candidates who would defend the interests of Garifunas. A professor said: "Since 1971 two new parties have arrived in Honduras:

The "Innovación y Unidad" and the "Demócrata Cristiano." Before, there were two parties only: "El National" and "El Liberal."

Professor Ambrosio Cacho from Trujillo who actually lives in Tegucigalpa and who has an active past as a leader of professors and students, has demonstrated how Garifuna groups prepared themselves before the election process. For example, "The Garifuna Association of Colon," was a political party organization in which the "minimum" plan included:

1. Conscious participation in the electoral process.
2. Political organization of the Garifuna communities of Colon.
3. Nomination of a Garifuna candidate so that he will be integrated in the future National Congress.
4. Increase of the self esteem of the Garifuna communities.
5. Incorporation of various professionals of Colon into this activity.

Objectives:

1. To contribute to the legalization of the citizenship status of 100% of the population.
2. To participate actively in organizations of the Garifuna of Colon community.
3. To coordinate six committees for the Department of Colon.
4. To choose five people as pre-candidates for the position of deputy.

Priorities:

In order to identify priorities for different communities one must present important projects to political parties.

The same professor demonstrated a wide cultural knowledge of the problems of the Garifuna. This was evident during his farewell address. He said: Before anything we want a national racial understanding with only one objective, to achieve later communication with other black groups of America and the world. The Garifuna is not an isolated group; we want to have a relationship with other black groups so that an effective exchange can exist.

OFRANEH

One organization that stands out in Honduras is the Organización Fraternal Negra Hondureña (OFRANEH).[2] In spite of some weaknesses and frailties this organization cannot be ignored because of its great success in polarizing public opinion and focusing it toward the Garifuna group of Honduras. This contributes to the birth of a "consciousness of a Garifuna town" with all its characteristics and demands, so that its voice could be heard. The Democratic representation had not been achieved through political parties, nor had these parties defended the rights and interests of the black population

Political parties are too busy looking for supporters and their votes. Therefore, they have no time to study cultural themes, neither to promote the identity of a group that wants to participate on the same level with other groups, in order to build a country where minorities can be integrated without disappearing as something worthless.

"OFRANEH was born fifteen years ago in Puerto Cortes City, Department of Colon, on the Atlantic Coast, in September, 1973. There was strong racial prejudice at that time in Puerto Cortes. I was in Costa Rica in transit to the USA, when the construction of Puerto Cortes docks was in its third stage. I was surprised by the fact that out of every 100 workers only four were Black. I began to seek information by asking people what we could do, but there was no

---

2. See chapter 4, page 53, footnote 9.

possibility that our complaints would be heard. Then, I wrote an article in a newspaper and announced it on the radio."

In that article don Erasmo Zuñiga pinpointed the existing racism particularly against blacks. The article was directed to the public at large, asking them to, at least, take positions. To religious organizations, he recommended to "dust the Bible" and do something; he addressed the governmental institutions saying that they should protect, enforce, and respect human rights. He reminded the black masses that "if they do not wake up, they will not even be able to catch fish for food because the cost of living was already too high." On the other hand, with obvious irony, he addressed the educated Garifunas who considered themselves better than the others because they went to school. He said to them: "You dear blacks, have you forgotten the miseries you left behind? Go back and remember them. Learn to build a country and do not act the way you are. . . ."

Mr. Zuñiga wrote the article to provoke a reaction among the educated people of his town, and make them recognize that all should face reality and overcome differences. It is in this sense that we should interpret the final sentence of his article: "I am neither black nor white, I am Honduran to the core."

Responses to his article were swift because the call was made at the precise moment. Some blacks began to meet to see what they could do, and an idea of a self organization with a central director emerged. The central director would begin to form groups in Garifuna communities on the North Coast of the Country. This project went into effect and the "Organización Fraternal Negra Hondureña," OFRANEH, is now present in almost all Garifuna communities. Shortly after his article two national meetings were organized. The governmental organizations trusted OFRANEH. That is why it was able to obtain economic help mainly from international institutions.

These contributions were made with the criteria of proper "development." But, on the other hand, great amount of unnecessary expenses provoked criticism; one example was the acquisition of a luxury vessel, expensive to maintain, which was used more by Ladinos than by Garifunas. No record of the expenses was kept and no receipts of payment were filed. In addition to futile expenses, there were also political rivalries. In fact, one director of OFRANEH was inclined toward the Liberal party, although the organization was not supposed to get involved in politics. These situations created serious internal conflicts that were impediments to successful initiatives.

At the beginning of 1985, the Second National Congress of OFRANEH confronted problems that caused divisions among valuable members. Erasmo Zúñiga explained the situation: "I do not see any progress in the Garifuna group. No one has expressed interest in the 'Black Town Conciousness' or offered any serious commitment to working toward this objective."

In order to find out what young professionals and Garifuna students who live in the capital, Tegucigalpa, think of OFRANEH, we spoke with some of them. The testimony of Roy Guevara, a law graduate and employee of "Consuplane," a state organization, was of particular interest. Roy Guevara is an articulate thirty-one year old young man, with a profound vision of OFRANEH; he believes that young and innovative forces even at the administrative level should be integrated into this organization: "In the beginning, the founding fathers incorporated OFRANEH into a developmental process through cultural demands; now young students and professionals aim for the same objective through a sense of development. In spite of internal contradictions that included ideologies, the most important thing to keep in mind is to consolidate OFRANEH. In addition, it is necessary for us to participate in the political process, so that we can intervene when it comes to making decisions. We also want to collaborate and progress with other ethnic groups which lack organizational representation.

It is important to define the true meaning of an ethnic entity and a national culture. Since we do not have an authentic inventory of national values, and we know that a town develops as it is conscious of its values and practices them, we must learn everything pertaining to us. For example, the Garifuna language should be taught in schools and universities. Research and development of projects should be conducted for each ethnic group.

It would be positive and important to attain more Garifuna political influence in the Department of Colon on the Atlantic Coast where the majority of the population is Garifuna. In the 168 years of the Republic we have not have one black representative. Now we have Dr. Ruben García Martínez from Trujillo. He is in the Ministry of Health but could not do much for us, perhaps because his power may have been very limited and subject to political pressures. Nevertheless, OFRANEH reaches beyond frontier lands.

Other Problems

As a group Garifuna commitment to assure recognition of its presence and opinion is necessary because, according to a leader of an institution for development, the political intentions of the government is to silence the Garifuna and other ethnic groups. Some groups have already been extinguished.

Another current problem is racism which still survives intensely in urban areas. The isolation necessary to maintain the culture of the Garifuna group intact is still an issue, even after efforts of new intellectuals and several initiatives to defend the cultural patrimony of the group.

The National Group of the Garifuna Ballet, directed by Mr. Armando Crisanto, a very friendly and enthusiastic person with a "Rastafarian" style hairdo, started certain initiatives. In fact, the actual ballet group of seventeen professionals has been recognized and sponsored by the Ministry of Culture and Tourism. According to Mr. Crisanto, "this group represents all Garifuna population through its history."

The Garifuna Ballet became well known in 1972 during the first Garifuna Culture Festival. Later, it was present in several black communities, from which several dance groups emerged. In 1983, the Garifuna Ballet had outstanding success touring Europe.

However, this caused dissatisfaction among the Garifuna. Some of them criticized certain folkloric expressions of the Garifuna Ballet as too commercial. For example, a Garifuna professional said: "The Ballet is deteriorating the cultural image of the Garifunas and gives us a bad image." Others added: "The Garifunas never had a ballet; this is a sign of acculturation which jeopardizes the

Garifuna traditions. We have to enforce our culture so that it does not become victimized by a foreign culture."

Young people ignore the Garifuna language. Schools teach only Castilian, a terrible way to destroy the identity of the Garifunas. Another aspect that should be considered is the big problem of losing the Garifuna lands because there are no land titles of ownership. Garifuna lands are being invaded by unscrupulous individuals, and the landowners are left with no means of subsistence, due to crop rotation, (they use soil in cycles moving from one site to another). The worst problem now is the presence of a Puerto Rican with U.S. citizenship who obtained a large tract of Garifuna land through illegal means. He negotiated with the Honduran government authorization to install a large military training and recruiting center for local and thousands of Salvadoran soldiers. The instructors were from the U.S. and the Salvadoran army. The facility was able to claim millions of U.S. dollars in reimbursements.

The Church and the Garifuna

What about the Church? What does the Church think of the Garifuna and in return, how do the Garifuna regard it? In the past, instead of having been in contact with communities promoting their organization, the Church was more concerned with enforcing the sacraments, and inculcating conformity, instead of facing real life problems. Although the Garifuna like to gather together for parties, when problems arise, they disperse and therefore need the guidance that only the Church can offer.

Monsignor Brufau, Bishop of Pedro Sula, recognizes that the Church has not penetrated deeply into the mentality and the evangelization of the Garifuna. He worries about current needs that demand pastoral attention. Unfortunately there is a lack of well educated people willing to help in these efforts.

CHAPTER 6

BLACKS IN NICARAGUA

A great variety of ethnic groups live on the Atlantic coast of Nicaragua, which covers 56% of Nicaraguan territory, but is only comprised of a total of 282,081 persons, less than 10% of the total population of the country. The density is four inhabitants per square kilometer.[1]

In general, public world opinion cared little about Latin American government treatment of their black populations. There was more concern for Indian population.

Miskitos

The Miskitos form the largest group on the Atlantic Coast of Nicaragua. They are already famous all over the world because of the role they play between the Sandinista government and the United States. Who are they? I asked this question several times to Honduran and Nicaraguan experts and the answers were always vague. The origin of Miskitos is still not very clear. The Miskitos, as well as the SUMU Indians seem to have come from one branch of the Misumalpan family. Among different groups belonging to this sub-group were the Bawihka Indians. It is commonly believed that during the Conquest era this Amerindian group bonded with African slaves or "cimarrones" (fugitives)[2] and with

---

1. See chapter 3, page 39, footnote 1.
2. Cimarrones: slaves who escaped from mines or from plantations. They formed towns by keeping their African traditions alive. See Introduction, page 6, footnote 35.

Europeans. The result of this mixture of races is perhaps the Miskito ethnic group. [3]

The name Miskito itself is of unknown origin. Zulema de Corrales, a Honduran anthropologist, said that "Miskitos" could be a derivative of the English word "muskets:" "fusil" or from "mosquitos" (zancudos) or also from the Miskito island. A young Miskito student stated that "Miskitos" is "an Amerindian group living on the Atlantic Coast of Nicaragua." It is historically known that they arrived from the North of Honduras. They live by hunting, fishing and agriculture. Thirty percent of Miskitos are black.

The most important detail about this group is that for over 300 years, it was practically dependent on the English. Beginning in 1690, English and Miskitos attacked Spanish cargo ships loaded with gold and spices in route for the mother country. The Spanish culture could not penetrate the Miskitos mentality because they were so strongly linked to the English that one Miskito leader went to Jamaica to be crowned king by the English governor. There was one president of Honduras who recognized the English power over the Miskito kingdom. The Mosco king expanded the Miskito influence from the Chiriqui Lake, in Panama, to the Chameleon River in Guatemala-Honduras frontier land. He was able to achieve this with British military and political support, and through business transactions including the sale into slavery of indigenous groups such as the Sumus and by the sale of agricultural products for the market.

A female teacher said: "The Miskitos are characterized by their speech; black or fair, they are recognized by their language." She added: "Therefore, to distinguish the black Miskitos from Black Creoles we wait until they speak."

The relationship between the Sandinistas, the Miskitos and blacks is tense. On the one hand, the traditional independence of the Honduran as well as the Nicaraguan authorities is based on the "cohesion" of the group. (We must not forget that it was only in 1860 that the USA forced England to stop interfering in

---

3. According to Ondina Castillo and Ricardo Zurita, a good portion of this information was taken from the first issue of *CIDCA*, Centro de Investigación y Documentación de la Costa Atlántica, and was completed with interviews of black Creoles, Garifunas, Miskitos and other informers.

Miskito affairs). However, the Miskitos were relegated to a reservation with their own chief. On the reservation the Miskitos enjoyed certain autonomy that ended when they were subdued by force in 1894 when President Zelaya was in office.

On the other hand, some mistakes were made by the Sandinista Governor who did not understand the reality of the Miskitos situation. In 1891, 21,000 inhabitants of Miskitos communities living along the Coco River (Honduran-Nicaraguan border) had to be dispersed because of constant attacks from the counter-revolutionaries. From this group, at least 10,000 crossed the border; 8,000 established themselves in the Tasba-Pril project and the remaining 3,000 went to Managua and other places. "According to a CIDCA[4] demographic study," the total population was 67,000 inhabitants, before the dispersion.

During this period the Apostolic Vicar Monsignor Salvador Schaeffer accompanied an exodus of Miskitos to Honduras and therefore became a target of criticism. This was an important fact for the Sandinista Revolutionaries who accepted that they made mistakes on the Atlantic Coast. Commander Thomas George admitted with honesty and courage the following:

The Miskito population has been totally involved in the struggle between revolutionaries and counter-revolutionaries. In the months following the revolutionaries' triumph, we knew very little about the aspirations of the ethnic groups of the Atlantic Coast. The revolutionary government had projects, and a lot of enthusiasm, but with little serious knowledge of town history. We wanted to change everything from one day to the next. Without thinking about consequences, we wanted to develop the Atlantic Coast with structures and projects similar to those already in place on the Pacific Coast. We ruined our good intentions with our ignorance.

The Miskitos did not understand the revolutionary changes. Parallel to a mutual lack of understanding between the Miskitos and the revolutionaries, are concrete facts for which we were responsible and we have accepted that responsibility. But the war situation in this frontier zone of the Atlantic Coast explains the errors and the deception.

---

4. CIDCA: See page 66, footnote 3.

In the same article, Thomas George insists that the U.S. administration took advantage of the difficulties in understanding the ethnicity and the origins of the Miskito population. The U.S. administration manipulated MISURASATA, an ethnic organization of the Atlantic Coast, created in 1979 by "the people of the Atlantic Coast,"[5] turning it into an "alternative" allied with the Contra Revolution. The Imperialist Strategy realized, at that time, that the National Sandinista Project not only misunderstood Miskito problems, but did not have much experience dealing with them. Therefore, the Imperialist Strategy turned these two issues into opportunistic tools to distort the Miskito reality at an international level. When the Miskitos crossed the Honduran border, they organized themselves into an army and the ethnic confrontation became not only a political but a military problem.

In any case, the Sandinista Government efforts to help the Miskitos with their needs and to support the population of the Atlantic Coast, were very strong with respect to health, education and agrarian reform. In spite of economic difficulties, the Sandinista government overcame the threat of an imminent armed invasion supported by the USA.

One Miskito who was living in Costa Rica with allied refugees commented: "The Miskitos have always been outcasts in Nicaragua; we thought that with the Sandinista Government things would improve, but the situation became worse. The Sandinista Government adopted a negative attitude towards us because we recovered our land."

"Now, in Nicaragua, there are senseless murders and many former prisoners seek refuge in other countries." He added that in 1981 in a clash with the Sandinistas, there were four deaths on one side and two on the other. The Red Cross and members of the Moravian Church interceded in favor of the physical well being of the Miskitos who had escaped to the jungle. The Sandinistas promised to let them go in peace. The Miskitos left, the others who participated

---

5.   These people sought to represent themselves through the creation of MISURASATA (Miskito, Sumo, Rama, Sandinista, working together) *www.ecm.de/cps/about_miskito.html*

in favor of the Miskitos were later captured and sent to prison. "We lost our trust in the Sandinista authorities."

Creoles

Black Creoles are a very important group on the Atlantic Coast of Nicaragua. They are descendents of colonial slaves and from the "cimarrones."[6] We should keep in mind that historically these blacks mixed with other local ethnic groups and with Europeans. As a result, this is a very particular ethnic and cultural group with African, Amerindian and European characteristics. This peculiarity can also be noticed in their language which is basically embedded with English vocabulary.

There are 26,000 people living in Bluefields, Corn Island, Laguna de Las Perlas and Puerto Cabezas, San Juan del Norte.

Blacks began to arrive in this area at the turn of the sixteenth century during the era of the Spanish Conquest. After that, they continued to arrive with pirates who frequented these coasts. Almost all blacks arrived as slaves, especially in 1630 with the formation of the English Company in Providence Island, which needed cheap labor. We should not forget that the black influence in this region was much stronger than the Spanish influence because of numerous English colonizers who arrived with slaves to populate and exploit the rich forest and agricultural zones.

In 1787 when England left the zone, some blacks stayed behind. Those who had bought their freedom and those who had escaped could stay if they chose and some did. Other groups of blacks, slaves of the colonizers, did not leave because their masters decided to stay. The emigration of Jamaicans from their country increased in the nineteenth century not only because of the increase in commerce but also because of other activities. They mixed with local Indians and whites becoming gradually more important until they were the dominant group of the social stratum of the coast.

---

6. See Introduction, page 6, footnote 35.

When U.S. companies were established in the country, especially in the banana industry, the need for manual labor increased, attracting the immigration of black Antilleans and blacks from the South of USA. They completed the formation of the "Creole" group.

Like the Miskitos, the Creoles also had to fight with the Sandinista Government, because, as one of them explained: "We wanted to do what we wanted and the Sandinistas wished us to do what they said." Now our social relations with the Miskitos and other Indians are good. Before, the Spaniards[7] were not allowed. Because of the unstable situation, they were kept away. Now, things have changed with the fact that blacks marry "Spanish"[8] women creating ethnic confusion. For this reason, some left their country and lived like fugitives in the mountains of Honduras and Costa Rica. Others have come together, especially through the MISURA group which was inclined toward the "Contras" for sometime when Brooklyn Rivera was the leader, but the majority became integrated into the mainstream and they will continue to do so if mutual understanding increases with government assistance.

The Creoles maintain that their English "Creole" language was influenced by other colonizers who wanted to communicate and do business with the English colonizers. It could be said that the Creole language is an English dialect strongly influenced by African accents and with contributions from the Sumu, Rama and Miskito languages.

Some Creoles earn a living from their businesses, others from hunting, fishing and agricultural activities, especially in the coconut industry. Among their typical dishes are: the "guagui," prepared with banana and coconut and the "rondon," which is salted meat seasoned with coconut.

---

7. Creoles called Spaniards to any mestizo not native from the Pacific coast.
8. Ibid. "Spanish" was term used by the Creoles to identify a mestizo who was not born in the Pacific Coast.

Garifunas

The Garifunas in Nicaragua are a small group of people and they are the last remnants of the large Garifuna population that spread from Belize to Guatemala, Honduras and Nicaragua. According to a CIDCA data there are 1,847 in total living in Laguna de las Perlas region in the following towns: Orinoco, La Fe, Justo Pint, Square Point and alongside the Wawasong River. According to reliable sources they arrived on the Atlantic Coast of Nicaragua during the most prosperous era of the banana industry and established themselves in Bluefields, where they mixed with the "Creoles." A Garifuna man said: "When our ancestors arrived here, they did not bring women with them; that is why they mixed with the local women: "Creoles, Miskitos, etc. and all lived in peace."

In contrast, the history of the Garifuna in Honduras is as follows: "A black leader, Gualumugu, who had been a soldier of General Francisco Morazán and who was living in Tocamacho, had an adoptive Miskito son, who was originally from the Miskito Island, Department of Colon. During a party this man got drunk and became involved in a fight. As vengeance, as soon as he had the opportunity he burned the house where the party was held. To avoid punishment he and his group boarded a ship sailing to Bluefields, where they settled." But according to a leader of OFRANEH, (Organización Fraternal Negra Hondureña), they kept in contact with the Garifuna group of Honduras, returning there for religious celebrations, especially for Holy Week, Christmas and for the "Day of the Garifuna" festivity. Since the Garifuna elders died, this small group of Garifunas has used the Garifuna language sparingly; therefore, at present the majority speak English "Creole," Spanish or Miskito.

Religious Aspects

The Moravian protestant religion predominates all along the Atlantic Coast, although there are also some Anglicans and Catholics. Particularly important are the Capuchin priests who, encouraged by the dynamic Bishop Salvador Schaeffer, made a commitment to work with the population. Numerous black women have joined different religious congregations and there are also black priests. A Garifuna man said: "Until now the Sandinistas have not interfered with our religious effort."

It is interesting to follow up on the development of the relationship between the Sandinista Government and the ethnic groups on the Atlantic Coast of Nicaragua. First of all, in Nicaragua the Sandinistas have been able to learn from past mistakes; more than in any other Central American country they are reflecting and working toward finding new solutions. It is also true that there still are groups who think that problems still in existence in Nicaragua are caused by social class differences. The Cultural Delegate of the Nicaraguan Embassy in Honduras said: "We cannot continue to only tell the story of our sufferings and cry over our miseries. Let's leave behind these issues and look forward to a bright future. We cannot satisfy everyone. We have to overcome exploitation by working on it."

There is also the issue of being faithful to the path of the oppressed population; they have become aware that one cannot really win the popular struggle based on social class struggle. Edmundo Garden Gitt, a Sandinista scholar, wrote:

> In a multiethnic society it is impossible to completely eliminate only one of these forms of oppression, while the others continue to exist. In strictly strategic terms, the success of a movement against any of these forms of oppression is debatable if it is not strategically supported by substantial parts of other groups. Therefore, what we need is a simultaneous struggle against all aspects of oppression for all movements involved in this fight. For ethnic groups, a simultaneous class struggle means to be aware of the social class to which we belong and to encourage the lower classes to become involved in the social class struggle against oppression. Popular revolutionary movements must be determined to end exploitation by dominant ethnic groups.

As we advance along this line of thought and actions, it seems to us that the Sandinista revolutions will be able to contribute positively to present day Socialism which has been hard on ethnic minorities particularly in strong regimes. We conclude with a quotation from the Editorial section of the Governmental Magazine *WANI*, July, 1984:

It is necessary to avoid the temptation of taking the easy way out, because it denies the historic and cultural diversity of the Garifunas instead of an incorrectly assumed cultural homogeneity: The challenge is to continue exploring socio-economic, cultural and political injustices inherited through centuries, and put an end to them. Only in this way will it be possible to build a new Nicaragua with the historical and cultural diversity of this polyglot and multiethnic society.

Religious groups, both theological and pastoral, should also accept this challenge and overcome never ending rivalries, sometimes fomented by third parties. We should recognize the contributions of both religious groups, so that we can progress with theological meditation and pastoral actions showing respect for Christ's presence in this country, oppressed because of its poverty and because of its blacks and Indians.

CHAPTER 7

BLACKS IN COSTA RICA

For a long time, Costa Rica has projected an image of a peaceful society, with its courteous, warm, work loving, and family oriented people, an island of peace in turbulent Central America.

We are not going to discuss the above comments, but it is enough to say that capitalism is comfortable here and on several occasions it has used this country for its own interests.

It could be said that we are dealing with a "totally O.K. country." That is why we wanted to learn the situation of blacks in Costa Rica and learn their history.

Although the black presence has existed in Costa Rica since the Conquest, during colonial times it was always limited. At that time there were no more than 200 black slaves in the country. One reason for the limited black population could be due to the lack of attention the Spanish paid to this region since it had no gold or silver. Few Spaniards and their families were dedicated to working the land. They avoided the unhealthy coasts and preferred mountainous zones, adjacent to the Central Valley, where until today, the most important cities of the country are settled, such as: San José, Heredia, Cartago, Pueblo de los Pardos, etc.

As plantations were small, one or two slaves were enough to work the land. In the Matina region the landlords preferred urban sites, and the slaves enjoyed humane treatment and a certain degree of freedom in the cities as well as in the country. Magnus Möner, a researcher, maintains that black slaves in Costa Rica enjoyed more freedom than slaves in other Latin American countries. This is a fact that differentiates Costa Rica from many other countries where mines and big plantations were a living inferno for Africans and their descendants.

In Pueblo de los Pardos the image of a black Virgin is named "La Negrita."[1] The statue was built by an artisan in 1635. The color of the statue is a symbol of a national effort to break ethnic barriers which still exists in some forms, in spite attempts to deter it.

The constant violent attacks from the "Zambos"[2] who dominated the North Atlantic Coast of Costa Rica and Nicaragua, were always an imminent danger during colonial times.

Land exploitation and coffee plantations created upward mobility. People had the opportunity to ascend up the social scale and slavery disappeared at the turn of the nineteenth century.

A slow manumission of slaves had already started in the eighteenth century and slavery as a social institution was dying. Therefore, to have household slaves became a luxury symbol.

According to Melendez, a historian, we must not forget that Juan Santamaría the national hero of Costa Rica represented "the descendants of the black colonials of Guanacaste mixed with the mestizos of Central Valley."

José Simeón Cañas, a Guatemalan priest, was among the main initiators of the liberation of the slaves which became law in all of Central America on April 17, 1824. In Costa Rica this law pertained to no more than 100 persons. At that time, the black colonial population of the North Pacific Coast, gradually mixed with local Indians, which resulted in the population of Guanacaste.

Antillean Blacks

Blacks from the Antilles, mostly from Jamaica, began to arrive in great numbers after 1872. They established themselves in the remote and deserted region of Limon, where the majority of the black population of Costa Rica is

---

1. Negrita: A loving black Virgin.
2. The Zambos in Costa Rica are the offspring of the intermarriage of Miskito Indians and Africans

concentrated. They came to work on railroad construction and in the banana plantations controlled by North American and English entrepreneurs.

The black Jamaican group was influenced by the absolute power of England. They were blinded by the attractions of the Great Empire to which they proudly belonged, to the point that they did not want to renounce the English language, "imperial" citizenship, or the "Jamaican" education of their children. The Jamaican attitude created resentment in the local ethnic groups of Spanish, mestizos, Indians and blacks. Jamaicans perceived themselves superior to the other groups.

They despised the Spaniards. There was a saying repeated by elder Jamaicans: "Los paña[3] tienen pielo," which meant: "The Spaniards have lice." They made fun of the mestizos who arrived from the mountains of the central region because they were sickly and easy prey to malaria and other diseases of tropical climates; Jamaicans considered them weak. Like all emigrants, Jamaicans had a dream of becoming rich and then return to their country. That is why they lived a kind of transitional life. Quince Duncan wrote: "They maintained a great devotion for the British Empire which transformed almost into a religion, developing in the individual a high degree of loyalty to the Crown that incapacitated him from identifying with other cultures."

This idealism became reality with the black laborers' relationship with an individual named Minor Keith, a U.S. citizen who pretended to be English. He was in charge of the railroad construction and sometimes could not afford to pay salaries to the workers, but under his promises, black Jamaicans worked even though he made them go eight months without pay.

Since coffee production was not enough to finance the railroad construction, Mr. Keith obtained large tracts of land concessions for a fruit company which later joined another similar enterprise from USA; this union developed into the famous United Fruit Company dedicated to the exploitation of the banana industry. This era is a nostalgic memory today for the black elders of Limon. They reminisce about the economic wellbeing of those years and the

---

3. Black Jamaicans, called Paña: or Spaniard to all non-black Jamaicans.

relationship they had with their English owners. The depression of the 1930s, the Second World War, the expansion of the Panama Canal, and certain restrictive governmental measures produced a tremendous socio-economic and cultural crisis that resulted in the exodus of Jamaicans to Panama and the USA.

Blacks paid a high price for this situation. They were discriminated against by laws and regulations; for example, one regulation prevented them from going inland beyond Turialba city.[4] Racism was a reality in Costa Rica, and the Banana Company that had exploited blacks so much, moved the center of its operations to the South Pacific zone of the country. Furthermore, on December 10, 1934, the Banana Company requested the President's signature to establish Art.5, Par.3, of Law 31 stating: "It is prohibited to employ black people in the production and exploitation of bananas in the Pacific Zone."

In 1948, the Civil War between Calderon and his opponent, Figueres, was declared. Blacks saw that Figueres treated them as Costa Ricans and spoke their language, therefore they voted in his favor. Figueres won the elections. He eliminated discriminatory laws and granted citizenship to Jamaicans. It was not that the former government did not want to grant citizenship to them, it was that the Jamaicans themselves did not want the citizenship until Figueres became interested in their situation. At the beginnings of the 1950s many blacks began to leave for the capital, San Jose, and other places in Costa Rica.

In the late 1980s the black population in the province of Limon was 17% of the total population of Limon. There must have been at least 40,000 blacks in Limon and we must not forget that many of them emigrated to Panama, to the United States and to other places of the country, especially to the capital, San Jose.

There are black authorities in Limon, and a new life has begun. Politically, the majority of blacks became allied with the Liberal National Party. On the other hand the Partido Auténtico Limonense of Marvin Wright was not successful because blacks thought that he was more inclined towards whites than to them.

---

4. Probably this regulation was not a law enacted by the government.

The Antillean group in Costa Rica is large and comprised of Jamaicans, but also includes those who came from French speaking islands and other regions. The black group identity was also supported by the presence of Marcus Garvey, the great Pan-African from Jamaica who on three occasions between 1906-1927 expressed thoughts that still encourage the black community of Costa Rica and of other nations. Now a pressure group has been created, thanks to the leaders that have emerged from the working class or from professional groups.

They have succeeded in placing representatives in the Parliament, almost all linked to the traditionally black Liberación Nacional party which has always opened opportunities to blacks at least in second place after whites. Blacks have also opened avenues into the local administration and into JABDEVA, the state organization, which was created for the development of the Port of Li

The image of blacks has improved on the national level. The organization of The Congreso Nacional of Afro-Costa Ricans, which took place in San Jose a few years ago, and the creation of the Afro-American professoriate are positive evidence of such improvement. Professor Eulalia Bernard, director of the Afro-American Professoriate, essayist and poet, said:

> Recently, I had an opportunity to watch the television program *Frente a Frente* in which Samuel Wilson, the Bishop of the Anglican Church, and Professor Javier Walter participated. The program was about the reality of Puerto Limon. A summary of this program would be: 'Puerto Limon produces wealth for the national government through agricultural exports, refinery of products and high taxes, such as the municipal taxes.'

On the other hand, in spite of the requirements listed by the authorities of the region and described in the documents "Limon Toward the Future," the government did not pay attention to us, or had developed an infrastructure that would allow the towns to improve their living conditions and to encourage the professionals to stay and struggle elbow to elbow with their people, instead of leaving for the capital. Costa Rica would have had advantages if everything would have been done for the sake of human and natural resources. The inhabitants of Limon proposed two solutions:

1). A plan of assistance with real opportunities for all, creating sources of work, especially in agriculture, tourism and industry. In this way one could see if blacks work or do not work. We need to make a decision to demand respect for our property and provide our lands with adequate protection against foreign invasion. We need political representation of our interests. People from Limon recognize that in spite of the existence of several political parties, union organizations, and religious sects, when the time comes to deal with strikes for common welfare, the population rallies together to fight for a common cause, overcoming divisions and differences.

2). An old idea with historic origins is: "separatism should be interpreted as regional autonomy with a sufficient economic base, or as an independent republic."

It seemed strange to me to hear such things on television, but after experiencing the reality of the black population of Costa Rica, especially of Puerto Limon, these ideas did not seem strange anymore. If the black group had experienced a long and difficult process in order to truly become an integral part of the national community, there is another long and tough journey ahead in peaceful Costa Rica.

Religious Groups and Organizations

Anglicans predominated in Limon because Anglicanism was the faith of the English in Jamaica. Private schools were run by Jamaicans, so that parents could educate their children with texts written in Jamaica using the English methodology. The influence of the Catholic Church has only increased substantially in the region in the last few years although the few blacks who attend the church are almost all women and children.

Limon is characterized by its religious syncretism. There are sects, loggias, fraternities and brotherhoods with special rites, surrounded by mystery attended exclusively for the initiated who are generally the affluent.

For example, for some "the Pocomia Fraternity" was not a dangerous organization. For others, it was a satanic cult group aiming to harm enemies whose leaders were feared by the people. One man said that in fact some strange things were going on in the meetings and that on several occasions the authorities had to intervene. Finally the leaders were expelled.

The "Obeah" expression comes from an African word meaning "power." It can be used "for protection and to harm others." Generally, it is used mainly in medical cases, and in spite of a defamation campaign, a lot of people visit the "curandero," or shaman. Awful things have been said about the "Obeah." It was even linked to human sacrifices. While some maintained that what was being said was true, others insisted that it was just a product of the popular imagination.

CHAPTER 8

BLACKS IN PANAMA

Panama is the Central American country with the largest black population. In this nation there is a polemic over culture, values, and "Afro" organizations.

Colonial Blacks

They are descendants of enslaved Africans who grew up in Panama during the Spanish Colony. They inherited the Spanish language and traditions of their masters. When Diego de Nicuesa, who came from Santo Domingo, arrived in the Atlantic Coast of the Isthmus of Panama, he founded the "Nombre de Dios"[1] city, in 1509. At least twenty black slaves were involved in the construction of the city fortifications. But soon the Spaniards realized that they would not be able to defend themselves from the diseases that quickly developed in these locations, so they left in search of better ones.

Then, on August 15, 1519, Pedrarias Dávila founded Panama La Vieja.[2] Until that time, few black slaves worked on the construction of public buildings, in the fields and in the households as domestics. But, when the Colony expanded toward the Pacific because of the discovery of the Inca Empire in 1526, Panama became an obligatory crossing site which gave the country the advantage of having a flourishing commerce accessible through the Chagres River and a route into the jungle that required a good number of stevedores; most of these men were blacks.

Businessmen used slaves instead of mules and preferred to keep the slaves for transportation rather than putting them to work in the mines because slaves

---

1. "Name of God"
2. Panama La Vieja; The Old Panama.

generated more profits. Blacks in Panama were at least lucky because they were not forced to work in mines as they were in other countries. There were more than 300 black slaves in Panama in 1530.

The Bayano King

Africans did not accept slavery as "normal" as some historians have said. The desire for freedom was always hidden in their souls and they took advantage of every opportunity to escape to the jungle. There, they found freedom. The Spaniards called their black fugitives "cimarrones." It was better for blacks to form groups and build small towns called "palenques" where they lived according to their customs and laws they brought from their countries of origin in Africa. They defended their lives with courage. Among the great leaders of the "cimarrones" are Felipillo and Bayano. The latter was a servant of the main house of the Real Audiencia of Panama. In 1549, when Mendoza, the representative of the Spanish King in Peru, was visiting, black Bayano overheard a conversation about the representative having in his hands a "Cedula Real"[3] to liberate the slaves. Bayano spread the news and with many other blacks sought refuge in the jungle where he was elected king. There, he and his people organized continuous assaults against the farms of the Spaniards and attacked the convoys that crossed their path on their way from the Pacific to the Atlantic. Several expeditions were organized to capture Bayano, but he was caught through betrayal. He was apprehended and sent to Spain where he lived at the "expense of the Crown." Even today, Felipillo and Bayano are the source of inspiration for blacks as symbols of the struggle against establishments that seem impossible to change. The "Cimarron" is an example of rebellion and the struggle for freedom which is the most sacred value and inalienable right of human beings.

---

3. Cédula Real: An order from the King of Spain to grant freedom to the slaves.

Pirates and Cimarrones

The slave trade took place during different periods under the Portuguese, French, and English. The Spaniards in a very limited way attempted to acquire their own slave trade enterprise, but they failed because they did not own slave "farms" in Africa. More importantly, they did not succeed because of the problems created by their numerous enemies in Europe and the difficult transportation between the Mother countries.

When the "cimarrones" escaped, they not only harassed the Spaniards with attacks, but also often became allies of the pirates who wanted the treasures accumulated in the Isthmus of Panama. Very often they assaulted the ships before the treasures were transported to Spain. They were also after the wealth of important businessmen of the city. For example, the pirate Francis Drake organized numerous attacks against Spanish ships. He died in 1597 from wounds he received during one of the assaults on Panama. A century later, Enrique Morgan is worth mentioning because he became famous for looting the rich city. These two were among the most well known pirates who needed the support of the "Cimarrones" or they would have not succeeded in their plans. The towns of the "Cimarrones," such as Matacin and Pacora, founded between the sixteenth and the beginnings of the seventeenth centuries, developed mainly because of the friendship between the black and the Indian tribes. The racial mixture favored demographic expansion. Some of these black towns disappeared with the construction of the Inter Oceanic Canal, but according to the Panamanian, Luis A. Diez Castillo, even today, "customs and traditions of black 'cimarrones' continue in Panama. In other words, they form part of the Panamanian culture."

Demographic Data

The presence of "colonial" blacks has also been of great significance in Panama. Let's consider the following demographic data from 1778: 3,474 slaves plus 33,377 "free colored people," in a total population of 59, 384 persons. From this total only one sixth was "white," one fifth was "Indian," which means that almost two thirds of the Panamanian population were of African descent. After

1809 there were no more slave cargo arrivals in Panama; therefore, the deplorable external slave commerce ended. But, the internal commerce continued until November 24, 1852, the date on which slavery was officially abolished in Panama.

Black Antilleans

Something that modified the internal relationship of the black population and also of the Panamanian nation was the beginning of railroad construction around 1850. This fact attracted a good number of blacks from nearby Caribbean islands. From 1870-1880 other Antillean emigrants, especially from French colonies, such as Martinique, arrived to work in the first stages of the construction of the Panama Canal which was under French supervision. In 1894, there were 18,000 wage workers engaged in this construction. Later, when the company declared bankruptcy, some of these workers returned to their islands, others stayed.

In 1903, when Panama became independent from Colombia, Panamanian enthusiasm for the canal returned. This dream for the canal became reality thanks to the economy and technology of the United States. One arrival after another of black workers from French Antilleans took place in Panama.

Later, as time passed, English workers became the majority of arrivals. Jamaica was the island that provided the most manual labor in Central American countries. One of the last Antillean immigrations from the Caribbean Islands to the Isthmus of Panama took place in 1939-1940.

The arrival of so many workers, mostly blacks, who came in waves to Panama, contributed to the construction of the Canal. Although the Canal was strategically important and convenient for the economy of the country, the presence of the black workers created social problems that marked the twentieth century history of the young Republic with social consequences from that time until today.

Antilleans struggled to claim working rights in the Canal Zone, where work security was at a minimum. According to George W. Westerman, one of the black Antillean leaders: "During the construction period, especially between 1904-1914, hundreds of black Antilleans died a violent death, or suffered permanent physical or mental injuries, due to premature or delayed dynamite explosions, asphyxia episodes, falls, rail derailment, land slides, rock slides and many, many more labor-related dangers."

Social Relations Between Antillean Immigrants and Panamanians

In addition to the hazardous work conditions, when it came to salaries, even with equal quality work, there were two systems of payment: "The gold roll and silver roll." The first one corresponded to white U.S. workers who had numerous social and economic advantages. For example, their salaries were double the amount for local workers. The second system "silver" was, in general, for the majority of the national workers and for the group who came from the Antilles. This system encouraged racial discrimination, because even the signs "Gold" and "Silver" appeared at water fountains, in public bathrooms, in post office windows, etc. This situation lasted until 1940! These differences were obvious also in lodging, food, school and education. In other words, this was a style of life that drove the Canal Zone to racial separation and prejudice that expanded to the United States.

In fact, at the beginning there was a policy accepting all immigrants without distinctions, but when Panama began to be recognized as a nation, a restrictive law was established almost immediately: in 1904, for Chinese immigrants; in 1913 for Syrians, Turks and North Africans, and in 1926 for Antilleans. This process culminated in the Panamanian constitution of 1941 with the triumph of the nationalistic political ideology, which together with other complementary laws, sanctioned differences based on race and skin color of immigrants, banning also certain employment positions and business possibilities, etc.

A "Denaturalization Law" was created to strip the citizenship of one million children of Antilleans causing serious difficulties for them. But we should not be scandalized only because of what was happening in Panama. There was also, racial discrimination at the same time in other countries of Central America: Guatemala, Honduras, Nicaragua, El Salvador and Costa Rica.

Racist Manifestations

An article published August 30, 1924, in *El Gráfico,* an influential weekly newspaper, gives an idea of the consequences of this racist mentality: "Antilleans crowding our inner cities lower our living standards and with their strange customs imprint the appearance of African cities in Panama, such as the cities of Colon and Bocas del Toro. This is among one of the most serious problems that this country must resolve."

In October 1940, several debates for constitutional reforms took place before the "Racist Constitution." The modifications aimed at the "non grata races." The Secretary of Justice and Government stated that Antilleans, mainly Jamaicans, "are not acceptable. Jamaicans cannot assimilate into the Panamanian population. One had never seen any Panamanian in an Antillean meeting because they cannot assimilate. I am sure that if we had a plebiscite, there would not be one Panamanian who would not question this vote for these "constitutional reforms." (There was a powerful ovation from the public.)

Juan de Arco Galindo, a black human rights defender, realizing that he was in the minority, said with bitterness: "Sooner or later we will have to retract and fix the damage that for no reason we have been causing to a large portion of the population, who always has outstanding behavior and has always shown examples of patriotism." The Secretary of Government answered: "It would really be a cowardly act of the Nation, if it retracts." But the Nation did retract on February 10, 1961, dissolving the law of discrimination.

Afro-Pan American Approaches

Taking into consideration the historic background, it will be easy for us to understand the position of blacks in Panama, as we can see in the September, 1981 *Memorias del Primer Congreso del Negro Panameño.* On that occasion, the Assembly affirmed that it was necessary to once again write the history of the black people, giving the names of black models and personalities of yesterday and today, emphasizing the economic importance of slavery and the contributions of black artisans and black artists to the national development, pointing out the global effects of the historic and ideological problems caused by racism from its origins to its global consequences.

The cultural aspect is very important because the African identity of the black is the key to an authentic progress. The following paragraph was written in the document:

> We must struggle against the historic tendency observed in Panama, to consider as national culture only certain manifestations of the central provinces; this is a hegemonic concept linked to a State control coming from the oligarchy, from which we have not yet been completely liberated. Our groups with their particularities and specific ethnic and social issues should search our history to reaffirm our identity through the knowledge of our roots, as well as recognizing the cultural expressions we have created in our lives in this environment.

There are divisions among black groups between conservatives and progressives, "bleached" elite and the masses. This situation does not contribute positively to the national economy, because cohesiveness and organization are needed in order to succeed as a group. "The majority of our people in our community, arrive here pretending to be cultured because they have attained certain level of sophistication. These people do not identify themselves with the black masses."

Black Groups

The solution to the problem should not come only from the "self declared" intellectuals, blacks or whites, but from the self commitment of the entire Afro-Panamanian ethnic group. Therefore, in an attempt to gain group cohesiveness several Afro-organizations emerged such as the APODAN, January 1979.[4] According to its founders, the Association serves as a union among black

---

4. APODAN, Asociación de Profesionales, Obreros o Dirigentes de Ascendencia Negra. (Association of Professional, Workers or Leaders of Black Ancestry). No information was found about the actual existence of APODAN.

Panamanians. In order to identify their needs, its members spread black Panamanian values, and their contributions to the national development allowing blacks to struggle elbow to elbow with other popular organizations for authentic social and global progress.

ARENEP[5] is another organization accepting ideological pluralism, by committing to change the negative image of blacks and by seeking all forms possible to achieve black unity. ARENEP combats all discrimination and stops the "waste of black brains," who contribute to the union of the Panamanian family. The basic conviction of this organization is "to be conscious of our own reality, which enables us to participate with dignity in the development of our country, Panama."

Afro Panamanians and the State

At the same time, it is required that the State modify its social integration policy, supporting not only the Hispanic-Indian culture, but also the African culture. Melva Lowe, a black spokesperson, said: "The country cannot afford to have discriminatory attitudes that cause significant loss of human resources." Black Panamanians do not want to be "invisible" anymore in the social structure of the country. They want to be recognized for their participation in the historical process, by including their contributions in school textbooks and by recognizing the importance of the English language that characterizes Antilleans in this era when the majority is bilingual.

The black community of Panama has progressed, inspired by the great black leaders such as the Pan African Marcus Garvey,[6] and much later by Jesse Jackson. Both have succeeded in encouraging this important strategic sector of Afro Americans from Latin America. But there is still a lot to do; there is a long

---

5. Accion Reivindicadora del Negro Panameño. (Action for the Revindication of Black Panamanians).

6. In 1916 Marcus Garvey founded UNIA, The Universal Negro Improvement Association, in Panama. During his visit to Panama he delivered speeches and stimulated the creation of work syndicates. He published the weekly newspaper "La Prensa" which lasted a very short time. Anthony Carver MacLean Hamilton, aamclean@panamwide.com.

journey ahead, not only from the perspective of the whites but also from the perspective of the black community.

In conclusion, Afro Panamanians want to be respected, and recognized by the society and by the State. This is a right that all citizens deserve, in order to be proud of their heritage, knowing that they have a lot to give and plenty to receive.

AFTERWORD

This book about the black presence in Panama, Costa Rica, Honduras, Guatemala and Belize, is the tip of the iceberg of the rich history of Africans in Central America. This translation from Spanish into English is an open window towards the African world in Ecuador and in Central America from its beginnings in the middle of the sixteenth century, until the last decades of the twentieth century.

The awakening of the black movement in South America, the Caribbean and Central America will be reinforced according to the degree of race identification. That is to say that ninety million people of African descent are in route to total liberation from discrimination. They will gain recognition for their contributions to the development and social transformation of their countries.

Niza Fabre

BIBLIOGRAPHY

Selected Bibliography in Spanish

Acuña, Olda M., and Denton, Carlos F. *La Familia en Costa Rica*. San José: Ministerio de Cultura, Juventud y Deporte e IDESPO, 1979.

Bardini, Roberto. *Belice: Historia de una nación en movimiento*. Tegucigalpa: Editorial Universitaria, 1978.

Cavero, Manuel. *Trujillo Trujillo*. Tegucigalpa: Editorial Guaymuras, 1975.
----------. *Mitociclo Trujillano*. Trujillo: n.p., 1978.

Cayetano, Sebastián y Fabián. *Los Garifunas*. Belize City: Mimeografiados Belize-City, 1984.

Conzemius, Eduard. *Miskitos y Sumus de Honduras y Nicaragua*. San José, Costa Rica: Editorial Libro Libre, 1984.

Diez Castillo, Luis A. *Los Cimarrones y los Negros Antillanos en Panamá*. Tudas, Panama: Imprenta Julio Mercado, 1981.

Galvao de Andrade Coelho, Ruy. *Los negros caribes de Honduras*. Tegucigalpa: Editorial Guaymuras, 1981.

García Murillo, Guillermo, and García Briceño, Luis Efrén. *Comidas y bebidas típicas de Guanacaste*. San José: Editorial Costa Rica, 1981.

Guzmán Navarro, Arturo. *El Istmo de Panamá: la trata esclavista durante el siglo XVIII*. Panamá: Editorial Universitaria, 1982.

Gutiérrez, Alfredo. *Manual Educativo Cultural Garifuna*. Tegucigalpa: Asepade, 1984.

Leiva Vivas, Rafael. *Tráfico de esclavos negros*. Tegucigalpa: Editorial Guaymuras, 1982.

McCaulay, Ellen. *No me hables de muerte . . . sino de parranda*. Tegucigalpa: Asepade, 1981.

Mariñas Otero, Luis. *Honduras*. Tegucigalpa, Editorial. Universitaria, 1983.

Miendez, Carlos, and Duncan, Quince. *El Negro en Costa Rica*. San José: Editorial Costa Rica, 1981.

Romero, Fernando, Dr. "El rey Bayano y los Negros Panameños en los mediados del siglo XVI" en *Hombre y cultura*, revista del Centro de Investigaciones Antropológicas, No.1, tomo 3, 1975, pp. 7-39.

Solien González, Nancie L. *La estructura del grupo familiar entre los Caribes-Negros.* Guatemala: Editorial José de Pineda Ibarra, Ministerio de Educación, 1979.

Wani. Centro de Investigaciones y Documentación de la Costa Atlántica (CIDCA), No.1, septiembre-diciembre, 1984.

Waterman, George W. *Los Inmigrantes Antillanos en Panamá.* Panamá: S. E., 1980.

Selected Bibliography in English

Buhler, Richard S. J. *A History of the Catholic Church in Belize.* Belize City: Editorial Bisra, 1976.

Palacios, Joseph O. "Carib Ancestral Rites: A brief Analysis" in *National Studies.* May 1973, Vol. I, No. 3, pp. 3-8.

Selected Bibliography in French

Wright, Tennant C. *"Petit guide pour le Belize,"* np : np, nd.

Works Cited

Bandelier, A. D. F. "Miguel Cabello de Balboa" in *The Catholic Encyclopedia.* Vol. III. Online Edition © 2003. Transcribed by Mathew Reak.

Cañizares, Raúl. *Cuban Santería: Walking With the Night.* Vermont: Destiny Books, 1999.

DRAE, Edition XXI. Madrid: Spasa Calpe, S.A., 1992.

El Habla del Ecuador. Diccionario de Ecuatorianismos. Quito: Universidad del Azuay, 1992.

El Negro en la Historia: Raíces Africanas en la Nacionalidad Ecuatoriana -500 años. Quito, Ecuador: Centro Cultural Afroecuatoriano, 1992.

"El País de los Incas: Época de la Conquista Iberoamericana," *La Historia y sus Protagonistas*. Ediciones Dolmen, 2001.

Escobar Konanz, Martha. *La frontera imprecisa*. Quito: Centro Cultural Afroecuatoriano.

Estupiñán Tello, Julio. *El negro en Esmeraldas: Apuntes para su estudio*. Quito, Ecuador: Gráficos Nacionales, 1967.

----------. *Esmeraldas de Ayer: Crónicas y anecdotario del pasado esmeraldeño*. Esmeraldas, Ecuador: REDIGRAF, 1996.

Garay Arellano, Ezio. *Varios Escritos Históricos de Guayaquil y su Provincia*. Guayaquil, Ecuador: Archivo Histórico del Guayas, 1999.

Martínez, Eduardo. *Cacique Tulcanaza*. Quito, Ecuador: Editora Andina, 1983.

Morel, E. D. "The Black Man's Burden," *The White Man in Africa From the Fifteenth Century to World War I*. Manchester: National Labor Press, 1920. BooksNet.Edition, 2001.

No Longer Invisible. Afro-Latin American Today. Ed. Minority Rights Groups: Minority Rights Publication, 1995.

Quintero, Dora. *Los espíritus del más allá. Diez personajes de la mitología afroesmeraldeña*. Quito: Abya-Yala, 1999.

Rueda Novoa, Rocío. *Zambaje y Autonomía. Historia de la Gente Negra*. Siglos XVI-XVIII. Quito, Ecuador: Abya-Yala, 2001.

"Spanish Colonial Era," U.S. Library of Congress. Countrystudies.us/ Ecuador/.htm

Whitten Jr., Norman E. *Class, Kinship and Power in an Ecuadorian Town: The Negroes of San Lorenzo*. Sandford, California: Stanford University Press, 1965.

Whitten Jr., Norman E., and Arlene Torres. *Blackness in Latin America and the Caribbean*, Vols. I, II. U.S.A: Indiana University Press,1998.

Zendrón, Claudio. *Cultura Negra y Espiritualidad*. Quito: Centro Cultural Afro-Ecuatoriano, 1997.

INDEX OF NAMES